Elvis - If Only We'd Known

To order additional copies, please contact us.
BookSurge, LLC
www.booksurge.com
1-866-308-6235
orders@booksurge.com

Elvis - If Only We'd Known

Sandra Richards
Edited by
Wendy Y. Tucker

2004

Elvis - If Only We'd Known

Introduction

Elvis's life has been told from many different perspectives—from the points of view of his ex-wife's, members of his entourage, and his fans. He was even the subject of a psychological assessment in *The Inner Elvis* by Dr. Peter Whitmer. But none of these analyses reach the depths that Elvis reached. In ecstasy and embitterment, Elvis lived outside the scope of the ordinary.

Elvis Presley's search for spiritual fulfillment led him to many different sources. He read the Bible along with other books, such as *The Impersonal Life, Autobiography of a Yogi, The Prophet,* and *Life and Teachings of the Masters of the Far East.* Elvis studied and practiced meditation and prayer becoming involved with the Self-Realization movement, visiting Daya Mata in a monastery, and talking with people who also were searching for the "meaning of life." Elvis even hired a hairdresser who studied metaphysics. Whenever Elvis had the opportunity, he asked spiritual questions of ministers and evangelists. He longed for the answers to his questions and continued searching for them until he died. The book, *The Scientific Search for the Face of Jesus,* was in his hands when he was found dead. But little did anyone know the lengths to which he would go in order to find the peace he searched for or the methods he would use.

Elvis wanted to be a teacher for God. He attempted to teach and talk about God to whomever he could; however, he was repressed, suppressed, ignored, threatened, and ridiculed to stop seeking the truth. Yet, in spite of all these negative influences and a lack of support, Elvis continued on his spiritual journey.

Because Elvis cannot speak for himself anymore, the biographies written about him are the medium through which his life's desire can be heard. All these stories declare what was most important to him—spiritual enlightenment. In these biographies, his voice is no longer silenced as family, friends, and fans openly talk about his spiritual quest and how much it meant to him. Although he believed his music was his greatest gift to the world, Elvis left behind an even greater contribution in his legacy of an unfulfilled spiritual quest.

Elvis was not a god to be worshipped, but a man looking for God to worship. Many times he was overheard declaring, "Jesus is King." If he were here, I believe Elvis would be pleased to know that his quest would inspire and encourage others to search for spiritual enlightenment. It is this quest that consumed his life. Elvis showed us that spiritual matters are so precious that they are worth searching for—even if it means losing our lives during that search. Elvis's life story of a quest for spiritual insight is a message of hope.

**

Author's Note: Elvis—If Only We'd Known *consists of true experiences. Relating these experiences is from memory and some material and circumstantial evidence. All opinions, judgments, conclusions, projections, and emotions are expressly mine with no malice intended.*
—*Sandra Richards*

This Book Is Dedicated To All People That Have Hopes And Dreams Of Their Own. May Courage Be Granted To Each One To Find And Fulfill The Purpose That God Has For Their Life.

Part I

Christian Values

Just about everyone knows who Elvis Presley was. His fame, fortune, and flaws have been the subject of countless books, newspapers, articles, and photography. Born Elvis Aron Presley on January 8, 1935, to a poor sharecropper's wife, little did anyone know what heights he would attain. Elvis lived the American dream. Though born into the home of the poorest of the poor, he used his God-given talent to become a household name.

Elvis was blessed from the day he was born. Not with worldly wealth, but with natural abilities and talents bestowed upon him by God. But, as we know, our lives start before we are actually born into this world. This is a strong biblical concept. When Samson's mother was told she would have a son, she was given instructions about what to eat and drink while pregnant (Judges 13:4, 5). And when Mary, pregnant with Jesus, went to visit her also-pregnant cousin Elizabeth, Elizabeth's baby leapt in her womb when Mary approached (Luke 1:41).

Elvis had some pre-birth experiences also. In *The Inner Elvis*, Dr. Peter Whitmer, Ph.D., speaks of Gladys, Elvis's mother, going to church at all hours of the day and night to listen to the preaching and singing. She also sang and danced along with the music. All this was part of Elvis's pre-natal experience—an experience of huge spiritual proportion.

As Elvis grew, he learned about religion by going to church with his mama. He enjoyed the singing and music more than the sermons. But along with the singing and music were the sermons. As he heard the pastor talking, the texts of the Bible were impressed upon his mind. Later in his life, he would turn to pastors and the Bible for answers when confused or unsure of his stand with God. Elvis wanted and needed reassurance of his acceptance with God. "'Elvis,' Pastor Hamell noted, 'was miserable. He prayed. We prayed. He prayed and wept. He asked me to forgive him for his sins. He didn't say what they were, and I didn't ask him what they were'" (Whitmer).

Although Elvis learned the importance of attending church, he also witnessed loved ones disregard the teachings of the church—a confusing message. His mother Gladys, for example, had violated the rules of conduct her church taught from the time she was a young girl. "The rules of the ... family's Pentecostal faith banned watching motion pictures.... When local entrepreneurs hung up a white sheet on the back of a flat-bed truck on Main Street in Saltillo for use as a movie screen every Saturday night, Gladys was sinfully attentive. In just a few hours she could go to church and be cleansed" (Whitmer).

Since Gladys was Elvis's only model for religious instruction from his earliest years, he accepted this double standard. With this example of conflicting standards, anyone would have become confused about religion. The church taught one thing, the Bible said other things, and his role models exhibited disregard for both. Later in life, Elvis would participate in adultery and think nothing of it. Why shouldn't he? After all, there was no hard and fast, "Thus saith the Lord" to follow.

That is not to say that God does not forgive. God is more than willing to forgive us for our sins. There is forgiveness without a doubt; there is also responsibility when sin is recognized. Once convicted of sin, we are to repent and turn away from it. God declares, "Again, when I say unto the wicked, Thou shalt surely die; if he turn from his sin, and do that which is lawful and right ... None of his sins that he hath committed shall be mentioned unto him. He hath done that

which is lawful and right; he shall surely live" (Ezekiel 33: 14, 16). God remonstrates that forgiveness is available, when the sinner repents and turns from sinning to following the requirements of God.

Elvis understood the importance of God in his life. He had heard passages from the Bible and sermons all throughout his childhood and youth. But he was surrounded by people that didn't take the Bible seriously. Elvis wasn't encouraged to delve into theological study. Even though Elvis knew "Church members 'are not to be conformed to this world,' nor were they to behave as nonbelievers do" and "Elvis would read the Bible every day of his life" (Whitmer), he had no concrete direction for his spirituality.

Evidently, swearing or using God's name in vain was not considered very important either. Elvis used God's name in expletives at least from the time he was a dating teenager (Whitmer). This blasphemy continued all throughout his life according to some of the biographies written about him. He is quoted using God's name in vain when he became angry in nearly every book written about him. This language must have been common with his family, friends, and the immediate community to which he belonged. This is apparent from the biography, *Elvis Aaron Presley—Revelations from the Memphis Mafia*, where Elvis's father, Vernon, swore while telling Elvis's grandfather that Jesse Garon, Elvis's twin, was dead. Elvis could only learn from what he himself experienced in his environment.

Besides this, Elvis lacked a strong father figure in his life. A basic understanding of God comes from having a loving, committed father who will support, teach and discipline his child, just as God does. Vernon was unable to provide that kind of environment for Elvis because he was missing from his son's life for many years. Vernon had been jailed for forgery and then remained away for years at a time. "As a father figure, he was the classic embodiment of everything not to be. He was disinterested in his family, emotionally distant, and geographically removed" (Whitmer).

In spite of all the conflicting views presented to Elvis, he somehow retained the desire to remain a Christian. In his heart of hearts he was drawn to spiritual matters. He began by attending church with his mother and continued to attend throughout his youth. It wasn't until his early twenties that he realized his church experience was not all that he thought it should be or could be. Elvis became disillusioned by clergy, by the lack of deep spirituality in his church experience, and by his own circumstances—especially after becoming wealthy.

Fame and Fortune

By the time Elvis was twenty-one, he was the most popular musical artist of his time. Enraptured by this success and unbelievable amounts of money, Elvis lived life to the fullest. Every physical desire, want, or need was readily complied with by everyone. The world was his oyster and nothing was withheld from him. After years of severe poverty and loneliness, Elvis was the center of attention in the known world. Not only was he applauded and heaped upon with adulation and adoration, but he also met with criticism, condemnation, and complaints. A generation of young people applauded and accepted Elvis while their parents and the previous generation denigrated his actions and sound. He was even burned in effigy.

Gladys had prepared her son for such attention. Since he had been the surviving twin of two boys, she had doted on him in every way, shape, and form conceivable. Elvis was primed for accepting the "worship" that came his way. It would have gone to any man's head. But with his extreme circumstances and overprotective care, Elvis became, and accepted, the position of "teen idol" to the masses of America's teenagers. As such, the world soon became his throne and he was worshipped for his talents. "Once again, he was the center of an emotional spotlight, recipient of a love that was as intense and abnormal as Gladys's" (Whitmer).

It has been said that absolute power corrupts absolutely. Elvis was no exception in his demands from the people around him. It didn't matter what hour of the day or night. If he just wanted his entourage to know he was up—that was the condition of being with him (Presley et. al.). He was the pinnacle of success. If someone didn't like being his paid slave, they could leave (Guralnick). And they could leave the girls, the money, the motorcycles, the cars, the clothes, the travel, and all the gifts he more than generously bestowed upon them. But in spite of all the material goods in Elvis's possession and all the attention bestowed upon him, he was still lonely, misunderstood, and unfulfilled. The power of his position only hid the need in his heart. To cover his naked pain, Elvis provided material things for the men he kept around him. He needed their acceptance because he was denied the spiritual acceptance that comes from knowing God and having God at the center of his relationships. "At the core of his need for this coterie were his feelings of insecurity and homesickness, a kind of vast and insatiable aloneness that could only be disguised, not dealt with" (Whitmer). Innately, Elvis knew he needed God's acceptance. He also knew he should conform to God's precepts.

When Elvis would reach out to men in spiritual positions, he still didn't get the emptiness within satisfied. Elvis reached a point where he didn't even want to go to church because he felt the preachers only wanted money from him. In Marty Lacker's book, he quoted Elvis saying, "'Every time I go to church, they have their hand out, wanting money.' Especially Reverend (James) Hamill, who'd been the Presleys' Assembly of God minister in Memphis" (Lacker, et al).

Then there were the fans. When Elvis tried to attend church, he couldn't because of the ruckus that the fans would make over him. Church services would be disrupted and Elvis stopped going out of consideration for the minister

(Whitmer). Fame and fortune have their price and Elvis was paying for his with the loss of spiritual support from the privilege of attending church.

Priscilla

Elvis was drafted during the Korean War and was sent to Germany after basic training for his tour of duty. There, he met a young teenage girl, Priscilla Beaulieu. His mother had just recently died, resulting in a huge void in his life. It wasn't unusual for Elvis to meet young girls, but in his vulnerable state, he became attached to Priscilla (Whitmer). Elvis soon became infatuated with her and they became very close. Every chance he had, they were together.

Elvis's tour of duty came to a close and he returned to the United States as a conquering hero. He was welcomed back with special recognition and soon returned to making more movies. Upon Elvis's discharge from the Army, he was forced to separate from Priscilla. This weighed upon him. He had formed a bond with her and wanted to have her with him. After many telephone calls to her father and all kinds of promises, Priscilla was sent to live at his home, Graceland, in Memphis, Tennessee. The years following were fraught with a tumultuous courtship.

Elvis evidently had promised Priscilla's stepfather, Captain Beaulieu, that she wouldn't be touched—and he kept his word. She had all of the physical, material things she could have wanted, yet the man of her dreams was out of reach. He was involved with dating other women, lying about it, and even turning his infidelity into outrage whenever she mentioned it to him (Esposito et. al.).

After Priscilla graduated from high school, Elvis procrastinated to marry her, even though she and her father were expecting wedding bells. Elvis was young, only thirty, and he still had the whole world at his feet. Women were throwing themselves at him, not caring that he might be engaged. He wasn't married yet! Maybe one of them could snatch him, if she was quick enough! Not only did the men in his life lack good morals, but the women around him—who should have been the ones to set the standards—were also too willing to "sell themselves" to be a part of his wild party life (Esposito).

Priscilla wasn't interested in spirituality. She was a healthy, young woman with the most intensely desirable man in the whole known world within reach. Her interest was in marrying and settling him down. She was willing to give up her own identity to please Elvis. He had her change her hair color, clothes, makeup, and the way she walked, talked, and lived. Priscilla lied about her age and where she was, as a teenager, to stay with him when they snuck away to Las Vegas while she visited him in California (Presley et. al.).

Besides that, why should she have been interested in Elvis's religious pursuits? He wasn't interested in her aspirations. Whenever she started a job, he told her to leave it. The only outside interests she was allowed were shopping and keeping Elvis's grandmother company. She was only there for him and his needs, whatever they were. After years of neglect, Priscilla had no desire to participate in his religious quest. She reacted quite normally by rejecting his religious ideals, just as he had repressed her aspirations (Presley et. al.).

On May 1, 1968, Elvis and Priscilla married at the Aladdin Hotel in Las Vegas. She became pregnant right away and exactly nine months to the day of their wedding, their daughter Lisa Marie was born. Elvis was temporarily faithful to Priscilla. But that didn't stop women from chasing him.

Elvis doted on his daughter and she became the light of his life. Yet, it was difficult to find time to be a daddy with such a busy schedule of concerts and movies. Priscilla couldn't be with him all the time, either. In the end, they led two separate lives.

Priscilla began taking Karate lessons and became emotionally and physically involved with her instructor, Mike Stone. Because Elvis was gone a lot and was involved with other women, Priscilla naturally had become lonely and wanted companionship. Less than five years later, Elvis and Priscilla divorced (Presley, et al).

Colonel Parker

Elvis was nineteen when he started cutting records professionally. At his concerts, his lean, lithe body gyrated and the crowds went wild. A young generation of rock 'n rollers were born. They started marching to the beat of a different drummer. As Elvis's popularity grew, so did the crowds that attended his concerts. Before too long, Elvis's manager, Colonel Tom Parker, scored some record-breaking deals for him. Of course, Parker benefited from his relationship with Elvis as well.

Colonel Parker became synonymous with Elvis Presley as the man behind "the man." Elvis began starring in movies, one after another, as they rolled out of Hollywood. America was hooked and so was Elvis. The fame and attention, the money and prestige, and all the things that come with popularity were his. He was the epitome of worldly success.

The next few years were turbulent ones. He made money, hand over fist, and spent as much as he made. Why not? There was plenty more where that had come from. Royalties and commissions poured in from his work. Even when he wasn't working, he had a steady stream of cash available for spending.

Colonel Parker was indeed making Elvis a star. Parker

gave one hundred percent of his time and talents to promote "his boy." But Parker wasn't interested in Elvis's spiritual quest, either. As a matter of fact, he was definitely against any spiritual interest Elvis had, knowing that Elvis could lose his total interest in secular songs, movies, and the wild worldly lifestyle he had been living (Stearn). Parker did everything he could to keep Elvis from experiencing a personal relationship with God. In the accounts of Colonel Parker, it is very clear that he was only interested in money. It was the driving force behind his compulsive-obsessive behavior in pushing Elvis constantly and not giving him the space he needed to fulfill his conscientious spiritual desires.

Although Elvis experienced great success and popularity in motion pictures and with record sales, he was still unhappy with his life. Elvis was grateful to Parker for getting him out of the gutter of poverty and into the glitter of popularity. Understandably, Elvis never wanted to be poor again. He seemed to fear being poor again. And yet, this fear became a reality as he neared the end of his life. In great distress over financial difficulties including a mortgage on Graceland, living expenses, handouts, and a large divorce settlement, Elvis was touring the country like a mad man the last couple years of his life (Whitmer).

Elvis's spending had also become unmanageable. He had a generous heart and knew what it was like to be without money. He bought great amounts of jewelry in his attempts to keep the people around him that he needed (Guralnick). He gave out money and gifts without considering the cost (Whitmer). His life became a constant round of tours, with short breaks in between. He had nothing else to live for. Yet, his current way of life wasn't worth living for, either.

Memphis Mafia

Elvis's entourage became known as The Memphis Mafia.
This group of men became his closest confidants. Just about
everywhere Elvis went, they were sure to go. On tours, around
Memphis, at Graceland, in Las Vegas or Hollywood, they
became recognized as Elvis's special group. Neither were
these men particularly interested in spiritual matters. They
were having too much fun having sex with every girl they
could in every city they visited and that came to Graceland
and Bel-Air to party with them (Esposito et. al.).These
married men denied their affairs to their wives.

Eventually, they lost any sense of wrong doing at all. They
convinced themselves that it was all right for them to commit
adultery—as long as it didn't ostensibly impact their lives.
Their wives were there for those times when no one else was
around to have sex with. As a matter of fact, they were less
faithful to their wives than to the girls that came and went.
"We were that ... ruthless, protecting each other because we
were cheating so much. 'Never, ever admit it,' Elvis always told
us. 'The girl can be there, right in front of her eyes, but never
admit it'" (Esposito et. al.).

And so began the conflict with Elvis—the struggle
between his spiritual quest and the pull of his friends and

the world. Elvis had said over and over again that if it weren't for the fans, he wouldn't have the life he was then living. He knew adultery was wrong, but he felt a responsibility to give his fans a piece of himself, even if it meant compromising his beliefs.

Everyone around Elvis knew of his interest in spiritual matters. For Christmas one year his friends bought him a white Bible with gold engraving on it (Lacker, et al). Larry Geller had been hired to talk with Elvis about metaphysical phenomena. As Elvis's spiritual guide, Geller was being paid more than the others, which caused problems, too. Elvis was willing to study these matters even though it made the Memphis Mafia uncomfortable. Elvis would talk to anybody and everybody about religion. It didn't matter where he was. It could be in his bedroom, on the set making a motion picture, on the bus traveling, or while eating (Lacker, et al).

Unfortunately, no one in Elvis's life really took spirituality seriously. Not even Larry Geller. For he, too, cheated on his wife while on tour with Elvis. No one in his life set hard and fast standards to live by.

The Fans

Elvis's fans hung around the gate at Graceland, his house in Bel-Air, or wherever he happened to be. Thousands of letters came every week—mostly from women—filled with sexual connotations. One evening, while going through some fan mail, Elvis winced after reading a letter written on toilet paper with "every conceivable unsavory word" on it (Stearn).

Although he received many disturbing letters and inappropriate fan letters, Elvis recognized that it was his fan's money that afforded him the prestige and lifestyle he enjoyed. If it weren't for them, he would still be a truck driver or possibly in a worse position.

Elvis loved his fans and wanted to make them happy. A few were able to get close enough to him to give him some happiness. One such fan was Frances Keenan, who wrote the book *Elvis You're Unforgettable*. While in Las Vegas, Keenan had a financial problem that Elvis found out about. He then paid for a room for her so she could stay. While there, Elvis visited her in her room. As they talked, he found a reason to pray for her, which greatly surprised her. Afterward, Elvis asked Frances what she wanted from him and she told him that she had always wanted him to re-enact a scene from a movie. Frances appreciated his re-creation of the scene, but she was moved by the longing that Elvis portrayed in his search for God's purpose for his life (Keenan et. al.).

Elvis would talk to other women who came into his life about spiritual matters. They would go into his bedroom—away from the Memphis Mafia—and talk for hours about God and Elvis's search for God's purpose in his life (Esposito). At the end of these conversations, Elvis would still be in limbo regarding his spiritual quest. Without the support he needed, Elvis would return to performing the secular songs that had become the bane of his existence to support himself, his family, and the many people on his payroll.

Searching for Spirituality

We are created with the desire to worship. Every culture in the world has some form of religion or beliefs to explain the beginning of life and the mystery of what happens after, or upon, death. Human beings are compelled to search for God. Elvis was no exception. "The spiritual side of Elvis was a dominant part of his nature" (Presley et. al.).

Smith stated, "It was like Elvis was searching for something.... He was looking for fulfillment. He starved for it and he was willing to experiment with a whole lot of things to find it" (Lacker, et al). Everyone around him understood that it was natural for Elvis to search for his relationship with God. However, he tried to practice his faith while maintaining unholy practices.

"Elvis had begun to smoke marijuana in the late sixties at our suggestion. We hoped it would help him sleep and he wouldn't need the pills, which he was beginning to use regularly" (Esposito et. al.). Even stoned, Elvis would turn to the Bible. In this state, he'd preach to whoever was with him. Apparently, he was trying to get them to want to study the Bible by smoking pot with them. If he compromised, then maybe they would too. Of course, he ended up swearing and adding words that weren't there. This brought gales of laughter to the men and women who were "high." He, too, lost the sense of the sacredness of the Holy Scriptures and fell among them laughing at his own corrupt improvisations (Esposito et. al.).

When the marijuana became boring, the next step was LSD (Presley et. al.). Elvis needed stronger mind-altering drugs to release the inhibitions of his naturally shy, quiet nature. His mind was constantly seeking stimulation and variety, especially when trying to understand his own higher purpose in life. That was how Larry Geller piqued his curiosity about metaphysical matters.

Having Larry Geller, his hairdresser, to discuss spiritual matters with, must have been such a relief for Elvis. Geller provided Elvis with an outlet for his desire to talk about religious themes. Geller also introduced Elvis to books and encouraged Elvis to pursue his spiritual goals.

The first day they met, Elvis asked Larry about his interests. Larry told Elvis about the different disciplines he was studying. They talked for four hours before being interrupted by one of the men who checked to see if Elvis was all right. After that first meeting, Elvis hired Larry to be his hairdresser and spiritual advisor.

Although Elvis studied with Geller for years, he never seemed to reach any kind of peace with himself. In *The Truth About Elvis*, Geller stated, "(Tom) Jones wondered why Elvis couldn't release his tensions through the meditations he advocated." Even people around Elvis noted that he was never content or at peace.

There was one incident while driving the bus across the desert when Elvis stopped the bus, jumped out, and ecstatically pointed to some cloud formations that had formed the likeness of Joseph Stalin. Larry Geller saw it too. Then Elvis saw a cloud shaped like Jesus. This experience reached Elvis's soul. He said, "My prayers have been answered. I have seen the Christ and the Antichrist, and I know what I have to do" (Stearn). When they arrived at their destination, Elvis was determined to leave show business and turn his life over to God (Guralnick).

This proclamation of spirituality overwhelmed and frightened Geller. As Elvis stated his intentions to follow God, all Geller could think was, "I've created a monster" (Geller). He was also afraid of Colonel Parker. What would happen if Elvis really did withdraw from performing? The whole Elvis empire could come crashing down and it would be all Geller's fault. So instead of acknowledging Elvis's spiritual awakening, Geller talked him out of it (Geller).

In *The Truth About Elvis*, Geller actually admits his fear of being blamed for Elvis's desire to change his life. "Larry was in a cold sweat. It didn't take much imagination to see how this latest stroke of news would be received by Colonel Parker and the others. Everything had been going smoothly until Larry turned up with his books and talk. Elvis had been making his three films a year, for a million dollars a picture and half the profits, one hit record after another, and now all this would be lost for a whim of the moment. He looked at Elvis, took in the sensuous face and eyes, the lithe, muscular body, the animated motions. Obviously, Elvis wasn't cut out for the monastery. At that moment, Larry knew he had to talk Elvis out of it, or else, he thought grimly, wind up in a monastery himself. He could see himself the object of total scorn. He made a silent prayer that God would make him convincing" (Stearn).

Elvis was drawn to the strict requirements of God. That was apparent when he started studying with Larry Geller, searching for the spiritual light that would fill the void in his heart. The void that no one understood. "Elvis ... wanted more time to devote to his spiritual studies and was impatient with the progress he was making" (Guralnick). And for a while, he abstained from having sexual relations in his desire to "overcome worldly temptations ... going through a cleansing period, physically and spiritually" (Presley et. al.). In reaching out for God, Elvis wanted to give up doing the silly movies and singing to please the crowds. He realized that the movies he made were not edifying or even good movies. But Larry talked him out of it by pointing Elvis to his fans and his "responsibility" to the world (Geller).

This had to be one of the final crushing blows for Elvis. He had trusted Geller with his mind and his heart. Elvis had opened up to him as he had to no other. Geller hadn't realized how purposeful Elvis had been in his searching. It became apparent that he didn't know what to do with the openness and honesty that Elvis was expressing.

A crisis was reached when Elvis fell and hurt himself. Colonel Parker ordered everyone away from him, especially Larry Geller. It was Parker's opportunity to capitalize on a misfortune, which was his forté. Soon after, Elvis, tired of fighting to defend his spirituality and the hopefulness it gave him, succumbed to the pressure and burned the books that were apparently causing such distress to the people around him (Presley et. al.).

Conflicts

In Elvis's search for religious meaning, he confronted conflicts continuously. The sexuality imposed upon him by his position as a teen idol caused great conflict within him. Over and over again in the biographies about him, the women who had the opportunity to be close to Elvis have stated that sex "just wasn't very important" to him (Guralnick). He could just as easily go without it as have it. Yet, because of his looks, money, and appeal to women, he was expected to behave as a sex idol and womanizer, whether he wanted to or not.

Elvis had been raised with biblical beliefs about sexual relationships. Part of him felt there was nothing wrong as long as the women involved were willing. However, another part of him struggled with the immorality of premarital sex. This was most evident with Priscilla Beaulieu, the teenager whom he met in Germany, who lived at Graceland for several years and ultimately married him.

Priscilla Beaulieu writes several times in *Elvis and Me*, how Elvis refused to have premarital sex with her. He wanted to make their first time special as husband and wife as he believed it should be according to the biblical standards he knew. Elvis should be given a lot of credit for his abstinence with Priscilla before marriage. Of course, he was having all kinds of illicit sex with just about everyone else at the same time; however, the right motivation was in his heart where she was concerned.

Elvis's mother had controlled his life from the time he was born until Colonel Parker came into his life and took control. "Elvis was controlled by his inability to take responsibility for his own life and for compromising his own standards" (Presley et. al.). But again, this is the way Elvis had been raised. Left to himself, Elvis lacked the strength to resist the popular route—the route that led to fame, fortune, and total acceptance by the multitudes.

Another conflict arose between Elvis's great respect for law, order, and policemen, and the drug addiction he found himself a victim of. In order to get the drugs, he had to break the law. Marijuana and LSD have both been quite openly discussed by several of the men that were in Elvis's entourage. These drugs are illegal. To add to his confusion, the police did not arrest him for possession or suspicion, even though they must have had information that he was using the substances. Joe Esposito, a member of the Memphis Mafia, tells of a visit to the jail in Palm Springs, Florida when they were "high" on marijuana, yet the police just smiled and gave them the peace sign. Elvis was allowed to break the law, which did not do him any good. He learned that he didn't have to be subject to the same restrictions others did, simply because he was Elvis, a world-renowned celebrity. These law officers didn't do Elvis any favors. They encouraged his drug habits by looking the other way and not stopping him.

All these conflicts stemmed from his strong religious background. One side was telling him, "It's alright. Everybody does it! You're Elvis Presley. You've earned the privilege of having as many girls and women as you want. After all, you're not forcing anyone to do these things with you. Yet the other side was telling him, "Elvis, you know the Ten Commandments. You know what fornication is. If you didn't, it wouldn't have bothered you to have sex with Priscilla before marriage. You know what the Bible says about the life you are living."

But then there were other factors urging him on. Hippies came and said, "If it feels good, do it!" "The new morality," came along. People were marrying and divorcing left and right. Nobody else was using any restraint and it wasn't expected of him. The men in his entourage gave him accolades and encouragement at the number of women with whom he was able to have sexual relationships. Promiscuity became the "norm" resulting in his conscience losing some of its conviction. And so the pressures kept building up. Elvis's religious beliefs slowly dwindled as he indulged in wild parties, drugs, a lack of self-control, and a smothered conscience.

Conflicts raged within Elvis. He was under the control of those around him. He was not the man that was portrayed to the world. He was insecure and unsure of himself. The only part of his life that he could control was the drugs he used and overeating he did to relieve his conscience. It has been documented that when a person overeats, the blood leaves the brain and goes to the stomach to digest the food. The mind becomes groggy and unable to function, much like alcohol's effect on the brain. The conflicts became too much to bear and Elvis escaped from reality to a *safe* place where he would not have to think about his unfulfilled spiritual and emotional desires.

Religious Freedom

This country came into being because of religious persecution. Pilgrims fled from the European countries that were hunting down and killing people that dared to open the Bible for themselves and seek the truth. Martyrs were burned at the stake, tortured in every conceivable way, and hounded and harassed in an effort to exterminate them from the face of the earth.

The Declaration of Independence contains the phrase "that all men are created equal, that they are endowed by their Creator with certain unalienable rights, that among these are Life, Liberty, and the pursuit of Happiness." It is the legacy of Americans to stand up for the downtrodden and offer freedom to all, especially freedom of religion and slavery. Yet, every effort Elvis made to increase his spirituality and practice his religious convictions was blocked. The one thing that made Elvis happiest was denied him by those he cared about the most and did the most for. Unfortunately, Elvis didn't understand about the laws that protect religious practices in this country and no one told him he had every right to practice and believe any way his conscience dictated to him.

During the growing pangs of the United States, we

suffered a civil war. The Northern States fought against the Southern States. The declared reason for the war was the holy cause of freeing the black slaves in the South. After the war was over, attempts were made by the government to enforce the freedoms of the ex-slaves with a military presence in the South—for a while. Eventually, they were withdrawn and the black citizens were left to the merciless persecution of their white Confederate slave owners again without recourse. Many black people were lynched, tortured, burned, shot, hung, and outright murdered for no reason other than having black skin.

At this time, certain men and women rose up in protest. Ida B. Wells wrote powerful descriptions of the atrocities being committed against her race. She told of the lies and the horrors that the people were made to suffer for trivial offenses. W.E.B. DuBois joined with others to organize the National Association for the Advancement of Colored People (NAACP) to end the discrimination and prejudice against African-Americans in finding jobs, housing, and property ownership.

In Elvis's case, there was no one to stand up for him at the time. No one was willing to fight the multitudes of fans, family, and friends who wanted to keep Elvis as the popular sex symbol he had become. He did not have the emotional and spiritual support he so desperately needed to make his own life fulfilled and happy. The loss of his freedom to believe and live his own spiritual dream was slowly taking his life.

Dimly Shining Hope

In spite of all the spiritual negativity that Elvis experienced, he remained steadfast in his belief in God. Every time he had the opportunity to talk about spirituality, the Bible, and the importance of God in his life, he did, even though those around him did not understand.

After Elvis's divorce in October 1973, "everything changed" according to Barbara Leigh (Esposito et. al.). Elvis had started to give up hope from what his biographies say. He lost interest in performing, which was the only thing he had left. During that time, he had to continue performing concerts to maintain his lifestyle and keep the favor of his fans.

Then, one day in the first part of 1974, Elvis received a letter unlike any he'd ever received before. It was handwritten by a young female fan. She simply said that she wanted to be his friend and signed the letter, "Your friend, Sandie." There was no last name and no return address. A couple of weeks later another letter arrived. It was again simple, with a joke about entertainers and signed the same way.

Over the next few weeks, Elvis received several of these letters. In one, she sent the Bible passage from Isaiah 40: 28-31: "Hast thou not known? Hast thou not heard, that the everlasting God, the LORD, the Creator of the ends of the earth, fainteth not, neither is weary? There is no searching of his understanding. He giveth power to the faint; and to them that have no might he increaseth strength. Even the youths shall faint and be weary, and the young men shall utterly fall. But they that wait upon the LORD shall renew their strength; they shall mount up with wings as eagles; they shall run, and not be weary; and they shall walk, and not faint."

Elvis became more and more curious about the writer of these letters, which were postmarked Glens Falls, New York. But without a last name, it would be impossible to locate her.

But then, she did send her last name and an address. Why? He didn't know. All he knew was here was someone interested in biblical ideas. Someone that even had the morals to say that she didn't believe in "one night stands." And she had even boldly said, "God wants us to meet this summer." She had a refreshing way of simple writing and in curiosity asked, "Do you ever get stage fright?"

An idea began to formulate in his ever restless mind. He would go to Glens Falls to meet her. He would go there because she probably couldn't afford to travel to Memphis. Glens Falls was a long way away. But first, he would hire a private investigator to locate her. That way, when they met, he would already know who she was and what she looked like.

Elvis became excited over this project. He started making plans, throwing himself into this project as he always did when something new and interesting was imminent like he did for the live telecast from Hawaii. "Elvis announced to the guys, 'I'm going to be the first to do a live show telecast by satellite!' We congratulated them (Elvis and Col. Parker), and Elvis talked exclusively about the project for days" (Esposito et. al.).

Elvis decided he would go with a gift. A gift unlike any he had ever given to any other woman before. Then he would surprise her with meeting him afterwards. His gift was to be a religious concert. He was sure this was the best way to present himself, for her letters spoke of her faith.

Elvis felt immense respect for this fan. She hadn't tried to proposition him and didn't want anything from him. She had only held out the hand of friendship. This concert would also cover his presence in Glens Falls. He remembered when, years before, he had gone to visit June Juanico at her home and the "yard filled with schoolgirls all there to gawk at Elvis who was hardly set up to be anonymous. He was really angry because he didn't have any privacy" (Whitmer). He didn't want to have the same problem this time.

In the letters, Sandie mentioned having read five etiquette books. She may not have been a high society woman, but she was trying to better herself. Elvis respected her for that. Elvis "believed that everyone had the potential to improve one's life" (Geller), and here was a young woman working on herself. He felt that there was a common bond between himself and Sandie. She was interested in spiritual matters as he was and she was trying to make her life better.

As the preparations were being made, Elvis lost some weight. Sandie had suggested that he get some exercise with his men to get into shape. She had asked, "What would we do without you?"

There is no way to describe Elvis's excitement and expectation about meeting Sandie. A suitable movie theatre, the Paramount, was located in Glens Falls for the concert. The setup was coming along nicely. The day before the concert was scheduled, some of Elvis' men arrived and took rooms at the Queensbury Hotel. It was their custom to go ahead of Elvis when he was going to be in a new place (Esposito, et. al.). It was their responsibility to locate Sandie and keep an eye on her movements so Elvis would know she would be at the concert.

Disappointment

When the men tried to locate Sandie's apartment, they found that she had moved. They called Elvis to let him know, but everything was in place for the free concert, which couldn't be called off at that point. At least they knew what she looked like, should she arrive, from the pictures the private investigator had taken of her without her knowledge.

On the afternoon of the concert, Sandie went to the park by the city library. She was sitting with a man who was lying on the ground near her. As they talked, suddenly, the man's body stiffened. A look of horror crossed Sandie's face as she realized he was having a seizure. Sandie was unsure of what to do, so she rolled him over onto his stomach to keep him from swallowing his tongue.

As she sat there, not knowing what else to do, three men ran up to help. One of them grabbed her friend in his arms and inserted a pen into his mouth to keep his tongue from getting swallowed. After a few tense moments, his body relaxed and the three men got up to leave. "Thank you," Sandie said, as they walked away. Soon after, Sandie and her friend got up to leave.

The three men watched they walked to the motel where Sandie was staying. Her friend left after escorting her to the motel. They wondered why she had moved out of the apartment she had been in.

That evening, Elvis waited at the Paramount Theatre for Sandie to appear. His men had spoken with some of Sandie's friends at the park earlier and found out that she was planning to go to the concert. As the time of the concert approached, Sandie still hadn't come and Elvis was getting anxious. At ten minutes before the concert was to begin, Sandie entered the building. Elvis relaxed.

There was standing room only by the time Sandie arrived. She didn't seem to be disturbed about standing through the concert. Elvis watched her during the concert. She was very interested in the young performer's explanation of how he had left a rock band to lead a Christ-filled life. Elvis asked the young man to sing one of his songs, wanting to see what reaction Sandie would have to it. As the song progressed and became drawn out, Elvis signaled the young performer to finish the song when he noticed that Sandie looked bored. The man ended the song, almost abruptly, and concluded by offering to pray.

The speaker said, "I'm going to kneel to pray. I know the floor is very dirty and I don't expect you to kneel." Suddenly, Sandie disappeared from sight. Elvis looked for her and then realized that she was kneeling for the prayer. Elvis kneeled too.

When the prayer was over, the people were invited to come forward to shake hands with the speaker. Elvis watched as Sandie made her way down to the front and shook hands with him. As she came back up the center aisle, he had one of his men stand halfway up the aisle with an offering plate, hoping to get her to stop.

As Sandie approached the man holding the offering plate, she avoided eye contact with him. When he unexpectedly spoke to her, Sandie reacted by swerving suddenly to the right, but turning her head to the left , and responding, as she continued moving up the center aisle. The man in the aisle turned to look at Elvis and shrugged his shoulders.

Thinking quickly, Elvis leaned over to his left to tell his stepbrother, Rick Stanley, to intercept her before reaching the door. Immediately, Rick started along the outer aisle meeting up with Sandie just before she was about to exit. Again, Sandie made a reply, but continued out the door. Elvis was puzzled.

When Rick returned he told Elvis, "I said, How do you do?" to her and she replied, 'Fine, thank you. How are you?' Then she just kept walking out the door."

"That's what she said to me, too," the first man chimed in.

Both men were surprised by Sandie's response. When replying to Rick, Sandie looked up at him with some of the bluest eyes he had ever seen with a quizzical look on her face. Rick was speechless at the glowing, happy face he saw. In spite of her friend's seizure in the park earlier that day, her face gleamed with happiness after the concert.

Elvis was confused by Sandie's response. He was sure that she had been approached appropriately. He had his men take him to the hotel where she was staying and sent a few of them to her room.

When they arrived, they could hear Elvis's record, "Let's Be Friends," playing through the door. The room was dark and quiet. They assumed she must be in bed for the night. They quietly talked about what to do. Should they knock on the door?

They may have reasoned, "She's awful young. Couldn't be more than sixteen years old. It's better that we not disturb her. Elvis doesn't need to get involved with any more young women. She's nothing but jailbait." Then they left.

Elvis must have been pretty disappointed. He'd spent time, energy, and money on the chance he would meet Sandie. Yet it had all been for nothing and he became depressed. He'd hoped and trusted that maybe Sandie could have helped him spiritually. She had certainly seemed to enjoy the concert. Elvis comforted himself with the belief that she had appreciated the concert, and if she was so young, it was better for him not to approach her. Elvis and his men left Glens Falls and went back to their lives in Memphis.

The Final Pleas

The next three and a half years for Elvis were fraught with hospitalizations, medications, nurses, pills, needles, and loss of hope and help. As the days went by, Elvis immersed himself in drugs and overeating. Because there was no one to understand and sympathize with his desire for spirituality, he clung to his beliefs within himself. Though repressed from expressing the deepest desires of his heart, Elvis continued to pray and forge ahead. He knew there were a lot of people counting on him for support and he took his responsibility seriously. He kept pushing himself to do the concerts. His body was still functioning, although at a greatly reduced rate, and his mind was closed and dying. He had no one to confide in. Even though Larry Geller was back with him, Elvis was still searching for spirituality, enlightenment, and the purpose in life that God had for him.

In April 1997, the last year of Elvis's life, Priscilla went to see him at Graceland after he had canceled a tour due to illness. In her book she wrote, "His curiosity for answers had not abated. He was still searching for his purpose in life, still feeling he had not found his calling ... But he never found a crusade to pull him out of his cloistered world.... That night he read to me, searching for answers, just as he had done the year before and the year before that and the years before that" (Presley et. al.).

Elvis's needs began to show in strange behaviors. He traveled to Washington D.C. to get a Federal Narcotics Badge from President Nixon. In speaking of this trip in *The Inner Elvis*, Dr. Whitmer said, "This weird brew of denial, projection, and grandiosity was really a cry for help that no one would recognize, let alone answer."

Elvis's fans saw him at concerts, yet didn't recognize his unspoken cry for help through his overweight body and frequent performance cancellations. Frances Keenan tells of going to Las Vegas for Elvis's concerts in August 1975. She had made her way up to the stage for a kiss and Elvis recognized her. They had exchanged a look that she interpreted as, "Mine had asked, 'What's wrong, Elvis?' and his had said, 'Please don't see the truth.'"

Unfortunately, no one did see the truth, Elvis was dying from lack of spiritual nourishment, and it wasn't his fault. He had tried over the years to obtain spiritual guidance in every way he knew how. He had gone out of his way to look for guidance and help.

Years after Elvis's death, notes were found written on Las Vegas Hilton Hotel stationery, "'I'm so lonely,' 'I don't know who I can talk to,' 'I can't stop ... I won't stop,' and finally, 'Prayer is my only salvation'" (Whitmer).

Elvis gradually went down the path of destruction. A combination of drugs, lost morals, and bad influences contributed to the deadening of his spirituality. Nonetheless, he kept searching and he held onto a little spark of hope that some way his dilemma could be solved. Was there no one he could turn to? Was the whole world so hardened by indifference to his needs that it didn't matter anymore?

Near the end of Elvis's life, he said from the stage in Las Vegas, "I don't want to be Elvis anymore." Wasn't anyone listening? Why won't anyone help me? he must have wondered. After all the years of giving, giving, giving to his fans, friends, and family, who would help him now?

In dark despair he searched his mind for something to grasp onto for hope. When hope is gone, all else is gone. Was there nothing to hope for? Maybe, just maybe, there was one who would hear and understand his need. It was a long shot, but when there is no where else to turn, desperate times demand desperate measures. Elvis was cloistered by the men around him. The cocoon he had created was becoming his death shroud. He had no one to turn to that he could trust with spiritual matters. Sandie was on his mind. Elvis reasoned that if she had been only sixteen three and a half years ago, she would be at least nineteen by now.

In Spring 1975, Sandie wrote one last letter, saying that she had reconciled with her husband and they now had a daughter. She had told Elvis, "I won't bother you any more." She must not have realized that he was at the Paramount Theatre that night in April 1974. Even though married with a child, she might still be willing to talk with him about spiritual matters.

At Elvis's last concert on June 26, 1977 he tried one last time to reach the only one left whom he thought could help him. CBS was filming a movie of his concerts entitled *Elvis in Concert*. Elvis knew he was losing the battle with his health and hope. In humility and self-abnegation before his audience of 20,000 fans, Elvis said, "I'm scared." He reached out in the only way he could think of to contact Sandie. He didn't care anymore what anyone else thought. He needed to have someone understand his desire and longing for spiritual fulfillment. Elvis finished his concert with the closing song "My Way" and left the building.

This wasn't the first time on the tour that Elvis had hinted at his fear. At the Pershing Municipal Auditorium, Elvis's opening remarks contained the following comment. "If you think I'm nervous, you're right." He was trying with all the available opportunities he had to contact Sandie.

Elvis wondered if Sandie would hear his answer to her question, "Do you ever get stage fright?" by stating, "I'm scared." All he could do now was hope that she would respond. He was sure the newspapers and celebrity magazines and papers would talk of his being scared. Elvis knew that Sandie had read these papers before. She had once read about a man in England that wanted to change his name to Elvis Presley which compelled her to write a vehement letter denouncing the man, telling Elvis that he should try to stop the man from doing it.

After Elvis's declaration from the stage, he felt that the tabloids would report it and she would read about it. She would know what he was trying to do. He felt it in his heart. She would come and help him if she knew it was all right for her to contact him.

Elvis was at the end of his rope and he longed to hear from this elusive young woman who possessed strong spiritual interests. He didn't quite know what had gone wrong when he had gone to Glens Falls to meet her. He had only the word of his men that she was too young and might cause trouble for him. Most of these men weren't his aides anymore.

Finally back at Graceland, Elvis spent six weeks waiting to see if a letter would come from Sandie. He watched the gate from his room, hoping against hope she would appear. He knew what she looked like having kept the pictures the private investigator had taken of her in Glens Falls three and a half years ago.

Elvis's next set of concert obligations was coming up and he didn't want to go. He felt used, misunderstood, and lonely. Yet the day arrived when he was to leave Graceland for the concert tour. He spent some time with Lisa Marie, his daughter. He played some racquetball and then he played "Unchained Melody" and "Blue Eyes Crying in the Rain" on the piano. Elvis went upstairs to his bedroom, intending to try to reach Sandie one more time.

Elvis had determined with the Physician's Desk Reference (PDR) how much of the prescription drugs his body should be able to handle without killing him. He wanted to get sick enough to have to be hospitalized again. He was so lonely he was willing to chance his very life in hopes of reaching Sandie and having her contact him again.

According to the "Unsolved Mysteries" episode that aired on November 6, 1997, in commemoration of the twentieth year anniversary of Elvis Presley's death, Rick Stanley admitted taking a dose of injections to Elvis and then a second one later. However, Elvis had saved the first one because he wanted to take them both together. When Rick went to Elvis's room, Elvis asked Rick to pray with him. He couldn't tell Rick or anyone else what he was going to do. He was scared, sick, and sequestered and felt that he had no one to turn to. Some of the men who had spent the last twenty years with him had abandoned him to write a tell-all book about his failures, faults, and flaws. While on his last tour, he'd become so out of it that a doctor had used a bucket of cold water to duck his head into so he could perform his useless and foolish songs once again. He didn't want to go through that again. All his searching had not produced any peace or hope. Nothing could ease the ache in his heart.

Elvis, the world's most beloved entertainer, lost everything that had ever mattered to him. His mother had died, his marriage had failed, and his attempts at spirituality had been repressed. Without spirituality and liberty, Elvis didn't want to face the life that had been carved out for him anymore. He wanted peace of mind and soul. He wanted to stop searching and actually find the answers to his questions. Maybe, just maybe, Sandie would write if he went into the hospital again and he was willing to risk overdose as a last-ditch effort.

Elvis didn't tell anyone what he was going to do, but in the Meditation Garden early in the morning of August 16, 1977, he said to Billy Smith, "'This is the most beautiful place in the world to me. More than any place I've ever been.'"

There was a soft smile on his lips and an almost ethereal look on his face. And then for no apparent reason, he turned to Billy and said, "'If I should die, Billy, don't grieve for me.

Let me go. Don't let your grief keep me earthbound. Let me go where I have to go'" (Stearn).

Later that day he was found alone and dead.

Sandie's Story

Part II

Prologue

Sandra sat on the floor of the living room playing. The television was on, but she wasn't paying any attention to it. Suddenly, music came from the television. She looked up to see a man in a black and white prison uniform sliding down a pole. He was singing and dancing around. Fascinated, Sandra watched the commercial for the movie, *Jailhouse Rock*.

Sandra couldn't believe the way the man was moving around. He was so free with his movements. Sandra felt uncomfortable watching him. Her family was strict conservative Christian and dancing wasn't allowed. In shock, she watched the commercial. That was her first sight and sound of Elvis Presley.

Sandra's rearing by a Christian family instilled within her the importance of God's standards. She became acutely aware of God's presence in her life. Secluded in quiet rural towns as she grew, she had no idea of the impact she would have on Elvis Presley before his death.

Peaceful Pastures

It was the summer of 1963 in Dexterville, New York. The meadow was a special place. Great spots of soft, green moss-like plants covered the ground in between grassy areas. Birds flitted and sang their songs, making the air pleasant with their music. Some apple trees gave a little shade The old broken stone fence surrounding the meadow lent a feeling of security as a ten-year old girl rested on a blanket, which she had spread on the soft green moss-like plants. Lying on her stomach, with her head resting on her arms, the warm summer sun made her drowsy and content. She came here to be alone. With two brothers and three sisters it was hard to find quiet sometimes.

As Sandra lay on the blanket, a silly thought came into her mind. She started laughing and her body bounced with every chortle. The harder she laughed, the more she bounced. She rolled over onto her back, then into a ball, still laughing so hard she had to hold her sides. Her private amusement was suddenly broken.

"Sandra, where are you?" her mother called. Sandra sat up, still giggling, and answered, "What?"

"Where are you?" asked her mother. Sandra stood up so

her mother could see her and picked up the blanket. "I'm over here." she answered as she started to leave the meadow.

Satisfied that Sandra was safe, Janette went back inside. Sandra made her way back toward the house. Her short reddish-brown hair framed a freckled face. Her deep blue eyes lent a thoughtful look to her young, somewhat impish face. Being a melancholy child, she loved it when she could be alone.

The family had moved just a few months ago into the small green house because the Seventh Day Adventist Church had a parochial school nearby. Janette and her husband Nathan had decided that they wanted the children to attend the parochial school. In the public schools dancing was taught in physical education and sometimes food in the cafeteria had pork in it. As Adventists, eating pork and dancing were forbidden.

Behind the house on a small hill, a great forest, filled with all sorts of wondrous things, waited for exploration. The children weren't allowed too far into the forest, for there was fear of bears and other animals which might be there. But Sandra liked to go to the top of the hill and explore. As long as she stayed within earshot, she was allowed there. An old logging road wound through, tempting her young feet to follow, and follow it she would, whenever she had the chance. There were still pools of water with frogs and soggy moss on either side of the road. Mosquitoes and other bugs buzzed around. Old logs, half rotted away, lay covered with moss and slime. The forest was cool and shady, offering solitude and peace.

On the right side of the house, a pine forest reached high into the sky. An old stone fence tumbled its way along the edge of the road in front of the pine trees. It was darker here and somewhat scary with the dead branches of the pine trees sticking straight out on the lower part of the trunks. Other dead branches twisted and turned looking like hands that could grab when passed by too closely. It was here that Gloria, her older sister, had teased Sandra and their brother, Dennis. Gloria had lured them into the pine trees and then ran off, leaving them alone to find their own way home. Sandra held Dennis' hand and sang "Onward Christian Soldiers" to bolster their courage as they picked their way out from the scary trees.

Sandra went into the house, took one of the ten volumes of The Bible Story books from the bookcase, and flopped down on her bed. She slept on a bed in the living room opposite the large wood-burning pot-belly stove. Her parents' double bed was also in the room. Brenda and Gloria, her two older sisters, respectively, were talking in the one other room used as a bedroom. Janette had started cooking supper and the aroma soon filled the small house. Tonight would be goulash and vegetables with bread and margarine. This was standard fare for the family. Sometimes meat and potatoes with vegetables were the choice.

Since dinner was being prepared, Sandra knew it wouldn't be long before her father would be coming home. She attuned her ears to listen for the car to come into the yard as she read. Her father worked two jobs and sometimes she didn't get to see him every day. With six kids to feed and another one on the way, he had to work two jobs.

The family wasn't rich, but they ate well and always had a home to live in. This house was rented. A car drove into the driveway. "Daddy's home!" Dennis and Sandra shouted in unison and headed for the door. Sandra left the book on the bed as she and Dennis ran to greet their father as he got out of the car. Walking back to the house, Dennis and Sandra chatted noisily as they walked beside their father, one on each side.

Inside, everyone was getting ready for supper by washing their hands. After everyone sat down Nathan said, "Let's say our blessing together. Bow your heads and close your eyes."

Everyone chorused, "God take this food that we shall eat and bless it, we shall break. Make all our actions kind and good, we ask for Jesus' sake. Amen."

That evening, Nathan took out his accordion to practice a hymn for special music in church that weekend. The accordion was overlaid with mother of pearl and the light danced across the white surface causing rainbows to appear from the movement. He'd had no formal training and played "by ear." Sandra was transfixed by the sight and watched as his fingers pressed the buttons and keys to make the music. She was disappointed when he stopped playing.

Sandra adored her father. She would follow him around when he was home. When Nathan had built some cupboards in the kitchen, Sandra could be found "helping" by handing him tools and watching as he worked.

When it was time for bed, they all took turns going to the outhouse, putting on their pajamas, and saying their prayers. The house soon settled into the peace and quiet of a sleeping family.

That summer proved to be the last normal one for the family. That fall, as if a harbinger of the future, President John F. Kennedy was shot in Dallas, Texas. Nathan called the children into the house to watch the procession saying, "You may never see anything like this again in your lifetime."

Sandra watched intently as the rider-less horse was led behind the casket. Thousands of people lined the streets to pay homage to their dead president. When the flag was presented to Mrs. Kennedy, Nathan told the children they could go outside and play again. Being a deeply thoughtful child, the impression of the procession remained with Sandra as she returned to the carefree play of a ten-year old.

Innocence

Mabel and Arthur Durgan, an older couple, were members of the church and good friends of the family. The family had lived next door to Mabel and Arthur before moving into the little green house. The Durgans had no children. With a large family next door, it was the next best thing. They were originally from Maryland and they both had slight accents when they spoke. Mabel was retired and loved to take long walks and bike rides. She often invited Brenda, Gloria, and Sandra to go along with her. Sandra was always ready to go for a hike.

The next summer, Mabel and Arthur came to visit one afternoon. After visiting for some time, they gave each other a quick glance.

Mabel asked, "Would you let Sandra spend the summer with us? Arthur will be working all summer and I'd like a walking companion."

Sandra nearly danced with excitement. She waited eagerly for the answer from her parents. Her mother and father asked her if she wanted to go.

"Yes!" she nearly exploded.

She was told to go pack some clothes to take. After being

admonished to "behave herself," she left with Mabel and Arthur.

Sandra was so excited. This was the first time she would be away from home alone. She was given a room upstairs all to herself. After having to sleep in the main room of the green house, a whole room to herself was bliss. She unpacked her clothes into the dresser and hung up her one Sabbath dress. Then she explored her new domain.

In the back yard was a huge mulberry tree that was perfect for climbing in, a picnic table, a garden, and a large backyard that was level for about 50 feet and then sloped down to a creek about 300 feet away from the top of the hill. All of this was mowed and considered part of the yard. Beyond that was a pine forest. Behind the house, a large garden interrupted the well-kept lawn. Green beans, corn, tomatoes, potatoes, peas and other vegetables flourished in the weeded and neat garden.

Inside the house, Sandra found a bookshelf. An avid reader, Sandra immediately selected a book and curled up in an armchair to read it after receiving permission.

Arthur came in the front door and went to the grandfather clock. He opened the door on the face and wound the clock with a key. Sandra heard the key winding in the clock and came out to see what was causing the strange noise. Before long, supper was ready. After eating and cleaning up the dishes, Mabel and Arthur went outside to sit at the picnic table near the tree. Sandra followed them outside.

Sandra wanted to climb the tree, but wasn't sure if it was permitted. She sat quietly listening to Mabel and Arthur talking, then, unable to stand it anymore asked, "Can I climb the tree?"

Arthur turned to her and replied, "Sure, just be careful you don't fall."

Sandra quickly climbed the tree, exploring and testing the branches for strength. The higher she climbed, the further away she could see. Looking to the north, she spotted a pony.

"There's a pony next door!" Sandra called out excitedly. Mabel and Arthur smiled. With a child around, this summer would be different.

Christian Values

Sandra woke to the bonging of the grandfather clock and lay quietly drifting in and out of semi-consciousness. Hearing movement below, her eyes opened to take in her surroundings. Suddenly realizing where she was, she sat up in the bed. Noises came from downstairs. Mabel and Arthur were talking in hushed voices, probably thinking she was still asleep. She listened for a moment then dressed and made her way downstairs.

"Good morning," Mabel and Arthur greeted her as the door opened at the bottom of the stairs.

"Good morning." Sandra responded politely, beaming happily.

"Breakfast is ready," Mabel announced. Arthur and Sandra didn't have to be told a second time. The table sat in a small alcove by a bay window. They seated themselves at the little table surrounded by windows. Arthur gave the blessing before they ate.

"So what will you do today?" Arthur asked Mabel.

"We will probably go for a walk to Phoenix," Mabel replied, turning to Sandra. "What do you think, Sandra?"

"That sounds like fun!" she replied. "I like to walk."

Arthur got up to leave for work. Mabel got up to give him

his lunch. They said good-bye at the door in the foyer by the grandfather clock. Sandra helped clean up the breakfast dishes and swept the floor. She wanted Mabel to let her stay for the rest of the summer. She was being as helpful as she could be. By 10 a.m., they were ready to go for their walk.

Phoenix was five miles away. Mabel and Sandra chatted as they walked. Mabel said, "Vacation Bible School starts soon. Would you like to go?"

"Yes," Sandra replied. "I like going to Vacation Bible School. I like to make crafts, sing songs, play the games, and hear the stories about Jesus. And we get a snack to eat, too."

Mabel laughed to hear Sandra going on and on about Vacation Bible School. Sandra was usually a pretty quiet child. She was two and a half years younger than Gloria and three years older than her brother Dennis. This left Sandra without a lot of companionship from anyone her own age. Mabel was surprised and delighted to hear how much Sandra liked Vacation Bible School. The church was within walking distance from the house. Mabel said she would help out with the program. This made the perfect combination for attending Vacation Bible School.

Sandra had already had a strong spiritual experience. When she was eight years old, she was playing a game with Brenda and Gloria. They were sitting on the floor of the porch between the beds. "The Old Rugged Cross" was playing on the record player. Suddenly, goosebumps ran all over her body and tears welled up in her eyes as Sandra envisioned Jesus dying for something He hadn't done.

"What's wrong?" Brenda asked, noting her expression.

Sandra quickly lowered her eyes and replied, "Nothing." She didn't know how to express her feelings and couldn't explain it to Brenda. Even though Sandra could feel Brenda's eyes still on her, she remained silent, and Brenda didn't ask again.

Sandra wished she had said, *"Listen to the song. Do you see Jesus hanging on the cross? Can you see Him dying with the crown of thorns on His brow? Can you feel the presence of the holy angels here in this room?"*

But fear can be paralyzing. She was afraid of being ridiculed, especially by her sisters. Although there should be no fear of ridicule from members of a family unit, it often happens, especially with children.

Sandra had experienced ridicule before. In the third grade, Sandra's physical education teacher made a point of letting the other children know she was different because of her religious beliefs. While in line during class one day, the teacher walked up behind her and booted her in the rear. It wasn't physically painful, bit it did make the others laugh.

Whatever he had expected, he didn't get it. For when he returned to the front of the class, she held her head high and looked straight ahead. Sandra detected surprise on his face when he looked at her. He never did that again.

"I am a soldier for Jesus," she thought. *"There were those in the Bible that were abused because they believed in God."* She remembered how Jesus sent an angel to rescue Daniel from the lion's den. It was an honor to be persecuted for Jesus.

Sandra remembered the fight that her father endured to keep his job when his company tried to make him work on the Sabbath. The union had sided with him and the company agreed to make arrangements for him to work other hours. Sandra's thoughts returned back to Mabel, who had been chatting as they walked.

"Yes, Vacation Bible School will be fun," Sandra thought.

Talking as they walked, Mabel and Sandra soon arrived at Phoenix, bought ice cream treats, and started home.

After arriving home, Mabel watched her favorite TV soap opera, "As The World Turns." Sandra went outside to climb the tree and wait for Arthur to come home. She found a comfortable branch and rested, enjoying the movement as the wind pushed it around lightly.

A few days later Sandra wandered out of the house looking for something to do. *"What should I do today?"* Sandra wondered. She climbed the mulberry tree and looked around. *"There's the pony,"* she thought. She watched the pony for a while, then decided to neigh to see if it would respond.

"Errrrhhhhhh, plllhhhrrrrr," she whinnied and snorted. The pony's response was terrific. His head came up and he whinnied in response. He looked in her direction and waited for another sound.

"Errrrhhhhhh, plllhhhrrrrr," Sandra replied. The pony started whinnying and running back and forth in his pasture.

"This is great!" Sandra thought. Sandra watched the pony going nuts trying to find the other horse he thought was over there. After a while, a woman came out of the house and yelled at her. She quickly hid in the branches of the tree until the woman went back into her house.

Sandra climbed down and went over to check out the garden. It looked like some of the green beans were ready to pick. She went inside and asked, "Mabel, may I pick some green beans in the garden?"

"Yes," Mabel replied and gave her a large pot to put the beans in. "Check the other vegetables and if any of those are ready, you can pick those, too." Sandra was delighted. She went to the garden and started picking the vegetables. Before long, Mabel came out to help with another pot. Arthur soon arrived home and he came out to the garden too. They finished picking all the vegetables that were ready.

After dinner, Sandra went outside to play. Someone walked along the road toward the house, but she didn't pay any attention to him. Soon Arthur came out and said sternly, "Sandra, my neighbor said you were teasing her pony today." Sandra looked sheepish.

"Don't do it again," he said.

"Okay." Sandra replied, watching him go back into the house. *"Gee, I can't get away with anything,"* she thought.

Parting

The summer sped by quickly with walks, bike riding, swimming at the beach, and grocery shopping. August arrived too quickly. The first weekend in August, Sandra, her family, and Mabel and Arthur were invited to another family's home for lunch after church. With lunch finished, the men took the children for a walk in the nearby woods. They followed an old logging road. When Sandra tried to hang with her father, he told her to go on ahead with the other kids. The adults were talking about something and they didn't want her to hear. Obediently, she ran and caught up with the rest of the group.

The following day, Mabel, Arthur, and Sandra went to pick cherries. They showed her which ones were just ripe enough for what they wanted. She was even allowed to climb a ladder to reach them. After picking as many as Mabel and Arthur wanted, they took the cherries home and cleaned them. That afternoon Mabel canned most of them.

On Friday of that week, Mabel made a cherry pie for dessert after supper. Sandra just liked to pick cherries, not eat them. Mabel had given her a piece of pie for dessert and she was trying to figure out a way to get around eating it.

As they were finishing their meal, her father arrived on his motorcycle. Mabel, Arthur, and Sandra went outside.

"Hi Daddy!" Sandra said.

"Hi, are you being good?" he asked.

"Yes Daddy," she replied. Arthur and Mabel both responded that she had been a good guest since being there.

Nathan was invited inside and offered a piece of pie. He noticed the uneaten piece on Sandra's plate.

"Eat your pie." he said firmly. Sandra wanted to please him, so she ate the pie, choking down every last bite. Nathan told Mabel and Arthur he was going into the hospital for an operation on Sunday. He had been having serious pain in his abdomen. After visiting for a short time, Nathan went outside to leave.

He was sitting on the blue Honda with the motor all revved up. Sandra asked, "Can I have a ride on the motorcycle?"

"Climb on," Nathan said. He gave Sandra a ride to the corner and back, less than half a mile away. When she got off she said, "'Bye, Daddy." He turned the motorcycle around and left. He waved his hand as he went. Sandra watched and waved until he was out of sight. It was the last time she saw him alive.

The Grim Reaper

Monday morning Mabel and Sandra went down the hill in back of the house to pick breakfast from the blackberry bushes that grew there. As they returned, with bowls brimming full of blackberries, Arthur drove into the yard.

"I wonder why Arthur is back," Sandra said as she and Mabel approached the house. When they reached Arthur, he looked at Mabel and then said to Sandra, "Sandra, your father has died." Mabel said something to Arthur and handing her bowl to Sandra said, "Take the berries to the house."

Sandra silently took Mabel's bowl and walked back to the house. Mabel and Arthur walked behind discussing something. Sandra cleaned and washed the berries, then put the bowls on the table and got out the milk. She waited for Mabel to eat with her. When Mabel came into the house, she told Sandra to eat breakfast, and then she and Arthur went into the living room to talk. They were very quiet and Sandra couldn't hear what they were saying. After breakfast she went up to her room and lay on the bed.

Sandra wasn't sure what she was supposed to do or feel. The realization of Arthur's statement hadn't fully penetrated yet. After a little while, Arthur left the house to go back to work and she went downstairs. Mabel didn't want to talk so

Sandra went outdoors where she watched the hummingbirds feeding from a feeder and remained quiet for the remainder of the day.

The next evening Mabel and Arthur were arguing. Arthur said, "She's old enough to go." Mabel answered, "I don't think she should." Arthur replied, "Janette asked us to have her dress in her church dress. It's up to her, not us, whether she goes or not." Mabel turned to Sandra and told her to put her church dress on because they were going out. Sandra was confused, but obeyed. She went upstairs and put on her light blue organdy dress with a full pleated skirt and black dress shoes. Arthur drove to a small building in the small town of West Monroe and they went inside.

Sandra was left to herself and wandered around looking at all the people. She was shocked to see Arthur crying. He looked at the other end of the room and when he did, she followed his gaze to see what was there. That is when she saw her father in the casket. In shocked silence she walked over to him. The sounds in the room became a blur as she focused on the figure in the casket. She could see the upper half of his body and he looked like he was sleeping. Inside, a red lining contrasted sharply against the white pillow his head was resting on. His hands were folded and when she saw them so still and white, she knew he would never hold her on his lap and he would never read to her again. That is when the full realization hit.

All of a sudden her mind was filled with the Bible stories of how Jesus raised people from the dead. She wanted to ask Jesus to raise him back up, but was afraid of what the others might think of her for asking such a thing. It was unheard of. She was afraid of being ridiculed if it didn't work. An overpowering feeling of hopelessness and helplessness overcame her.

Suddenly Sandra started sobbing uncontrollably. She'd never cried so hard in all her life, not even when she'd been spanked. Nathan's sister, Aunt Marguerite, took her in her arms and tried to comfort her by saying, "He isn't suffering anymore." Sandra didn't even know he had been suffering.

Sandra cried and cried and cried at the funeral parlor and was finally taken out of the viewing room into a small office where the funeral director offered her a plastic rain bonnet to shut her up. She even had her choice of colors. In painful agony, she realized that everyone wanted her to stop crying, so she repressed her tears. She stayed in the office until time to leave with Mabel and Arthur.

Sandra looked at the plastic bonnet in her hand and thought, "I don't want this. I want my daddy."

When they got home, Sandra was totally exhausted from the crying. She wearily took off her dress, hung it up, put her pajamas on, said her prayers, and went to bed. That night she slept fitfully and kept tossing around. Early the next morning, she fell out of bed. Mabel and Arthur's bedroom was directly underneath and they heard her land on the hardwood floor. Arthur called up through the ceiling, "Are you all right?"

Sandra answered, "Yes" and climbed back into bed. That was the one and only time she'd ever fallen out of bed.

The next day was the funeral and interment at the cemetery. After entering the funeral parlor, Arthur led Mabel and Sandra to seats about halfway from the front of the room. Sandra sat with them, not knowing she was supposed to be in the front row. One of the funeral attendants came to her and asked if she wanted to sit in the front.

Sandra answered, "No, because I will start crying again." If they didn't want to hear her cry, she wouldn't, but she could not bear to look at her father like that. They left her where she was. Thus, Sandra learned to repress her feelings to keep from imposing on others.

Sandra kept her eyes averted from the casket. After the sermon, she went directly out to Mabel and Arthur's car and waited for them. At the cemetery, she stayed near Mabel and Arthur until the casket was put over the hole on the boards. When that happened, she walked to the back of the group to be by herself. As the minister spoke, she found comfort in the sunshine and soft breeze. *"Now I have to take care of myself,"* she thought. *"My mother has four kids smaller than me that she has to take care of. I am on my own."*

After the service, Janette told Sandra she was moving the family to her mother's house in Stillwater, New York. She asked, "Do you want to go with us or stay with Mabel and Arthur until school starts?" Sandra replied, "I'd like to stay with Mabel and Arthur if they want me to."

Sandra was relieved. She wouldn't have to be around all the other kids and go through the moving process again. She remembered what a confusing mess that was. This would give her a little more time to deal with her father's death and to brace herself for the future.

Living with Grandparents

Janette's mother and father, affectionately called, Mommer and Poppy, lived in a small house on the bank of the Hudson River. It seemed that Poppy was gone most of the time. He worked as an engineer driving trains to and from Maine. Sometimes he would be gone two or three days at a time. Mommer didn't work and she helped Janette with the children.

The house was overflowing with children and their paraphernalia. Sandra longed for the quiet of Mabel and Arthur's house. Although she was with the family, she was detached.

Sandra wandered outside where Brenda and Gloria were riding a bicycle. The driveway was a large U-shape and they were taking turns with the bicycle. Sandra asked if she could take a turn. Brenda and Gloria exchanged glances, then said she had to wait until they each took another turn. Sandra waited patiently until they both had ridden slowly up and back.

"It's more fun if you go fast," Brenda said, as she handed the bicycle to Sandra. Sandra rode the bike up and back then waited as Brenda and Gloria again slowly took their turns.

Realizing she wasn't wanted, Sandra wandered away. It wasn't worth the aggravation to fight them over the bicycle.

Going onto the screened porch, Sandra sat on the glider and watched the river flow by. Dennis came out of the house and saw Sandra on the swing.

"Do you wanna go swimming?" he asked.

Turning toward Dennis she eagerly replied, "Yeah, let's ask Mom if we can."

After getting permission, along with the perfunctory "use an inner tube and don't go out too far," they put on their swimsuits and went into the water. It was especially fun to float on the inner tubes when the boats went by and made waves to bob around on. Poppy kept an area in front of the house free of seaweed so they wouldn't have to walk in it.

A small rowboat with an outboard engine sat covered nearby. Only weeks after her father's death, Sandra remembered him taking Dennis and her out in the boat and riding up and down the river. He had made waves then turned the boat to cross the waves. The action had jarred Sandra, but no complaint escaped her lips. Then they had landed on the sandy shore by the bend to skip stones and build castles in the sand. Sandra quickly averted her eyes and followed Dennis out into the water. She didn't want to cry in public again and be repressed for showing her emotions.

A couple hours later, Mommer came out. "Sandra, Dennis," she called, "time to come back and get ready for dinner. Stay outdoors until you've dried off." Then turning to face Brenda and Gloria, she called them from their bike riding. Mommer went back into the house as everyone started heading towards her. Dennis and Sandra raced back, kicking, splashing, and yelling that each would be the first one back. Sandra let Dennis win. Besides, this way she could be in the water longer. They put their inner tubes under the porch where it cantilevered over the bank of the river. Mommer had left towels at the top of the stairs that led to the water. After drying themselves off, they hung the towels up on the clothesline to dry. Supper was buffet style because the kitchen was very small. The older children went outside to eat on the porch.

There were only two bedrooms in the house and everyone had been assigned a place to sleep. Sandra had to share a day bed with Dennis. They slept head to toe. Brenda and Gloria shared a bed and the three younger children slept near Janette so she could hear them if they woke up in the night. The house quieted quickly once everyone was in bed.

Sandra said her prayers while lying in bed by silently talking to God. Since her father died, her mother was extra busy with the children and family prayer time had somehow been skipped. Having said her prayers for blessings and forgiveness, she went to sleep.

Memories and Moving

Janette woke early-another day to face with seven children. She loved them all, but she wondered how she was going to be able to take care of them. Baby Janet stirred in her crib. Janette got up and watched her for a moment. She picked up baby Janet and changed her diaper, then carried her to the kitchen to make her cereal and feed her.

Janette's thoughts continued, remembering the sequence of the children's births. Brenda and Gloria were only eleven months apart and they had paired off together. Sandra had been born next. She had been a quiet child, drawn to her father, following him around whenever he was home. *"She blames me for her father's death,"* Janette thought. *"She's so withdrawn."*

Janette thought about Sandra's birth and how she had originally chosen Beverly for her name. Then Eleanor, Nathan's sister, named her baby girl Beverly, who was born three months before Sandra. Janette looked for another name and chose Sandra.

Janette's reminiscing continued. Dennis was born almost three years later. Named Nathan Dennis after his father, they had decided to call him by his middle name to eliminate confusion. He, too, had clung to his father whenever he was around. Naturally, Dennis and Sandra had formed a bond, as Brenda and Gloria had.

Five years later, Sharon had come along, who was born on Sandra's birthday. *"We gave Sharon Sandra's initials,"* she mused. *"A year and five months later Michael was born, and fourteen months after that Janet had arrived. Then when Nathan died, I thought I was pregnant again. Thank you, God, for not letting me be pregnant again,"* she prayed fervently.

Janette remembered an incident from when she was a teenager. She was sleeping in bed and as she turned to lie face down, an unseen hand pushed her head into the pillow as if to suffocate her. She prayed silently with all her might and when the pressure released from her head, she sat up gasping for air. Janette wondered why that memory flashed through her mind.

Janette finished feeding baby Janet the cereal, then took her back to her crib. After putting Janet down, Janette started getting the rest of the kids up. She would do whatever she had to for them, and that included putting them into a Christian school, even if she couldn't afford it. Janette was going to take Brenda, Gloria, Sandra, and Dennis to school registration at the nearest Seventh-day Adventist school. The principal had already told her that no children would be turned away. Some of the other church members would help pay the tuition through donations for families that couldn't afford the whole amount. Janette was taking him at his word.

Soon everyone was fed and dressed. Janette's mother, Goldie, would be watching Sharon, Michael, and Janet while the others were registering for school. Brenda, Gloria, Sandra, and Dennis were loaded into the car. Brenda and Gloria were eager to meet new kids. Sandra sat quietly in the back seat with Dennis, who was trying to have a conversation with her. She answered him with monosyllables. Janette caught Sandra's eyes for just a split second in the mirror before Sandra looked away. *"What is she thinking?"* Janette wondered. Mabel and Arthur had wanted to keep her, but

Janette wanted the family together. *"Maybe she is wishing she was with them,"* Janette thought. *"I wish I knew her better."*

Arriving at the schoolhouse, the kids piled out of the car. The school had three classrooms with three teachers. Mr. Kaiser taught the ninth and tenth grade. Mr. Borgersen taught fifth through eighth grade. Mr. Lehrer taught first through fourth grade. Each child met with their teacher and was assigned a desk.

Other parents were there with their children. Gloria and Brenda were soon talking with some of the other children. Sandra found a swing. Dennis struck up a conversation with some of the boys. The registration process didn't take very long and soon they were called to come to the car. It was time to leave.

A New Home

The family stayed at Mommer's and Poppy's house until November, when Janette located and bought a home in Fort Anne. The old farmhouse had been owned by an elderly couple who were members of the Adventist church. Janette picked up the four children at school and drove out to the house.

"We aren't staying at Mommer's anymore," she announced. "I've bought a house and we are going there tonight."

Sandra's interest was piqued. She waited impatiently to see the new house. When they drove into the yard, she wasn't disappointed. A column of smoke wafted from the chimney of the old farmhouse. A tree in the front yard had a U-shaped branch from other kids climbing in it and already had her invitation written all over it. A barn sat at the end of the driveway.

"Okay, everybody out," Janette said.

Brenda and Gloria got out, each carrying a child. Sandra and Dennis walked up to the house and they waited for their mother to open the door. Janette unlocked the door and said, "Take your boots off and leave them on the porch. Then come upstairs and I'll show you your rooms."

They trooped into the kitchen where the staircase wound

in a semi-circular curl up into the second floor. The steps were in need of paint. The old wooden steps creaked as the horde of children ascended.

Once upstairs, Janette assigned the rooms. There were four rooms that could be used as bedrooms. One of the rooms was currently being used to house the clothing for the Community Services of the local Adventist church, so that left three other rooms for use.

"Brenda and Gloria get the biggest room because they have to share. Sandra, you have the small room and Dennis, you have to sleep in the hallway during the winter. Your bedroom has no heat duct in it and it's too cold for you to use it now. The other bedroom over there is being used for clothing for the Community Services of the church," Janette said. "Your clothes are in your rooms. You need to put them away." Then she went downstairs with Sharon, Michael, and Janet.

Sandra started opening up boxes and putting her clothes in the dresser and closet. Soon Dennis was at her door.

"Can I come in?" he asked.

"Yes, come over and look out the window," she replied. "There's a barn that is ours and that fence must be ours. Dennis came in and looked out the window at the barn and fence.

"I want to go meet the kids down the road," Dennis said.

"You better ask Mom if it's okay," Sandra said. "If you wait, I'll come with you."

After finishing their unpacking, they went downstairs to the kitchen. Dennis asked, "Can we go down the road and play with the kids we saw?" Janette replied, "Not tonight, you have homework to do, it's dark outside, and it's almost time for supper. Get started on your homework." Sandra and Dennis exchanged glances and then went upstairs. Dennis was muttering under his breath something about homework.

Sandra went into her room. She could hear Brenda and Gloria talking in their room. They had always been together.

She felt left out of their relationship, but comforted herself with the fact that Dennis was always willing to be with her.

Brenda and Gloria stayed in their room as long as they could. They knew as soon as they were done, they would be expected to help with the younger children. It wasn't that they minded, but it was just nice to have some privacy away from everybody else. After all, Brenda was only fourteen and Gloria thirteen. They were just adolescents themselves. They divided up the room so each could have their own area for personal belongings.

"I'm glad we got the room with the door on it," Gloria said.

Brenda replied, "Maybe we can keep the other kids out of our stuff."

Gloria went on, "Boy, that Randy sure is cute," referring to one of the boys in school.

"He is the best-looking one in school," Brenda agreed. They giggled together as they unpacked.

Gloria picked up a skirt and looked at it. "This one is getting too small for me," she said.

Brenda replied, "I have some that are too small for me, too. I put them over there. We can give them to Sandra to wear." Gloria tossed the skirt onto the pile Brenda had started.

"Okay, we'll give them to her later."

Brenda stacked the empty boxes inside each other by size. "Let's stay here until we get called for supper," she suggested sitting down on her bed. "Besides, we have to get our homework done. If we go downstairs, we'll have to watch the kids."

Gloria agreed, "Yeah, I know." She finished with her boxes and sat down on her bed facing Brenda. "Let's take a break before starting our homework," she said, then stretched out on her bed. Gloria didn't like school or homework. She worked hard for every grade she got. Gloria had to repeat a grade once and she didn't want that to happen again.

Brenda and Gloria could hear Sandra and Dennis

throwing their boxes down the stairs and then taking them out to the shed. Then they climbed back up the stairs talking together.

Their mother called upstairs, "Come on down for supper."

Sandra and Dennis were quick to put away their homework and run down the stairs. Brenda and Gloria followed, carrying the empty boxes from their room. Sharon, Michael, and Janet were already eating as they arrived. They put the boxes into the shed and returned to eat supper with the rest of the family. There wasn't a lot of conversation at the table. After supper was finished, Brenda, Gloria, Sandra, and Dennis had to finish their homework and then settle down for the night.

When Sandra had said her prayers, kneeling by her bed, she lay down and covered her head with the blankets. She was afraid of the dark. In church she'd learned about evil angels and how they had supernatural powers. But, she'd also learned about the holy angels that God used to protect those who believed in Him. Sandra believed that she had her own guardian angel. As she drifted off to sleep, she could feel the presence of her guardian angel in her room. She felt protected and safe from the evil angels.

Early one morning Sandra woke up from a bad dream. She had stood outside the little green house in Dexterville, New York. Her father rode up, parked his motorcycle, and then walked toward the house. His eyes stared straight ahead as she watched him walk stiffly past without noticing her.

Sweating, she woke up and lay in the dark, terrified. *"What if an evil angel impersonates my father?"* she wondered. Sandra understood the state of the dead. In church she'd heard the text expounded upon over and over again. "The living know that they shall die, but the dead know not anything" (Ecclesiastes 9:5). It wasn't possible for her father to contact her. If there was an appearance by him, it could only be done by the angels of Satan.

Stories of people that have seen family members after

their deaths have been attributed to after-life existence. *"But the Bible is very clear about what happens to people when they die. It was just a bad dream. I need to go back to sleep."*

A Safe Harbor

Even though Sandra was a natural tomboy, she still enjoyed going to church. On Sabbaths that her mom didn't go to service, she'd ask Mr. and Mrs. Taylor to pick her up on their way there. They drove through Fort Anne on their way to church and didn't mind stopping to get her. Mr. and Mrs. Taylor were the couple that had sold the house to Janette.

Sandra felt uncomfortable with her peers. Instead of going to her youth class, she preferred to sit in the back of the adult class and listen to them discuss their weekly lessons. Every quarter of the year, a new quarterly was handed out with lessons for each week. The lessons were studied individually during the week and then discussed as a group on Sabbath morning. All the divisions, including the Cradle Roll class (infants to four years old), had lessons each week.

The youth class received a weekly magazine entitled *The Guide*. Besides the lesson for the following week, there were stories of other children and the problems they faced with articles that depicted the dangers and horrors of drugs, alcohol, and tobacco.

One such story was about a teenage girl that decided to try LSD. The story told how the girl had taken LSD, and after it had taken effect, she was heard screaming. People rushed to see what was wrong and found her screaming, "Get them off. Get them off me!" She thought she was covered with creepy crawly spiders and bugs. In her effort to get them off, she was taking a razor and scraping the skin off her arms and legs. Chills ran up and down Sandra's body.

"How could anybody take drugs and do that to themselves?" she thought. *"What a horrible experience to go through."* The story stayed with her. She determined to never use drugs. She didn't want her mind altered in any way.

Church was very important to Sandra. As far back as she could remember, she and her family were in church every week, unless someone was sick. One of her strongest memories was being in church as a family with her father.

The church had youth social events requiring high moral standards. No smoking, drinking, make-up, or jewelry was allowed in church or at school. Dancing was forbidden too. Sandra liked the standards of the church. It gave her definite guidelines to go by, although it sometimes created problems with other kids her age and gave them an opportunity to tease her.

In the fall the church organized a hay ride and a corn roast. For Halloween, the children in the Pathfinder Club would go door to door requesting canned food for the church's food pantry for Thanksgiving and Christmas baskets. Volunteers from the church ran the Pathfinder Club, which was similar to the Boy and Girl Scouts in activities, honors, and ranks.

Ice-skating parties were hosted by members who would clear the snow off a frozen pond for the young people to skate on. There would always be hot chocolate and some kind of snack to go along with it. Most of the time, Brenda, Gloria, Dennis, and Sandra would ride with other church members to get to the functions. It was too hard for Janette to dress three small children to take the others to functions and then go out to get them late at night.

The church would get the youth to put on spaghetti dinners or have a lunch-box social where special lunches were auctioned off to raise money for a project.

The church was a haven for Sandra. It nurtured her spiritually and she felt accepted there. She wanted to be in church every week that she could. However, there were times when no one could take her because they were out of town or were visiting another church that week as a family. On these Sabbaths, Sandra would go for long walks along West Road. A couple of times, Brenda and Gloria would walk with her around the circle that West Road made by connecting with South Bay Road in two places. It took a few hours to walk the circle, as it was several miles long. Brenda and Gloria mostly talked between themselves, occasionally turning to speak to Sandra or make a comment about something. Sandra kept silent most of the time, unless she saw something interesting and then pointed it out to them. She was happy just to be walking with them. At least she wasn't alone for a few hours.

If Sandra was alone, she would hike in the woods or sit by the waterfall and sing hymns. She liked to sing when alone the hymns she knew by heart, but she made sure no one else was around to hear, for fear that she would be ridiculed. At the end of the Sabbath, she'd go home for supper. Sometimes the television was on and Sandra would sit and watch a little of it before going upstairs to bed.

Growing Pains

For the next school year, Janette enrolled the children in the Fort Anne public school. She felt uncomfortable having the other church members pay the tuition for her kids.

Sandra was thirteen and in seventh grade. She liked Danny, one of the boys in her homeroom class. He was good looking and had dark hair. She thought he liked her because he had written on his desk "Sandy." When she confided in one of the other girls about what she thought, the other girl told Danny. He stood up between classes and said, "That's not your name on my desk. That's Sandy Hill."

Sandra was embarrassed and hurt. A pang went through her heart. She'd never experienced that feeling before. She turned bright red, hung her head, and concentrated on reading the book on her desk. She determined not to confide in anyone again.

Later on in the year, a school dance was being held. Some of the boys started whispering. Danny stood up and looking at Sandra said, "Sandy, will you go to the dance with me?" Sandra replied, "I don't dance." Some of the others snickered. A couple of days later, he did it again. Sandra gave the same response with the same results. What could she do to stop being picked on about this? She decided to ask Brenda what she should do.

Sandra looked up to Brenda a lot. She was smart and willing to help her sometimes. Even though Sandra didn't try to intrude in Brenda and Gloria's close relationship, she wished she felt more welcomed by them. There were times when she didn't know how to do something and she'd turned to Brenda for advice. This was one of those times.

That night at home, Sandra knocked on Brenda and Gloria's door. Gloria opened it.

"Can I come in?" Sandra asked.

"Sure," Brenda said.

Sandra explained why she was interrupting them. "I have a problem with one of the boys at school. He keeps asking me to go to the dance with him. I told him I don't dance, but he won't stop. What do I do?"

"Who is it?" Gloria asked.

"It's Danny Hall," Sandra replied.

Brenda looked at Sandra and said, "Tell him yes."

Sandra looked at her incredulously, "Tell him yes?"

Brenda replied, "Yes, tell him yes."

Sandra looked dubious, "Are you sure that's what I should say?"

"He's just teasing you. If you tell him yes, he'll leave you alone." Brenda explained.

"Okay, if you think it will work, I'll try it," Sandra replied and left the room. She was still doubtful it would work.

The next day, sure enough, Danny asked her again, "Will you go to the dance with me Sandy?" Sandra looked him in the eye. She thought, *"What if he expected me to go to the dance because I say yes?"* Her heart was pounding in her chest, but the word came out calmly, "Yes." Sandra put an inflection of acceptance into her voice and face. Danny's face changed suddenly, as if caught off guard. Mr. Kazlo told everyone to sit down. Danny took the opportunity to get into his seat and face towards the front.

Sandra thought, *"It worked. It really worked. Now he will leave me alone."* She couldn't believe it was so easy and she was so relieved. That night Brenda asked her what happened.

"I told him yes and he stopped asking me," Sandra answered triumphantly, yet still incredulous that it had worked. She smiled at the recollection, "Thank you for helping me."

"That's okay," Brenda said.

Brenda felt good about helping her little sister with this problem. Sandra was usually quiet and didn't cause any trouble in the family. She thought Sandra liked being distant from her, and if that was what Sandra wanted, then she wouldn't push herself on her. Brenda was happy that she could help her out with this problem.

A Stepfather

A few young men started coming to the house to court Brenda and Gloria. Sandra always thought that Brenda and Gloria were much better looking than she was and they seemed to know how to dress and what to do around boys. Even though Sandra didn't know how to interact with boys on all levels, she preferred being around them and having them as friends. Girls were gossipy and liked to talk about other girls. Boys mostly talked about guns, cars, trucks, fishing, hunting, and other things like that. It wasn't interpersonal stuff, which is what Sandra had such a hard time dealing with.

Ralph, who was the oldest, had short brown curly hair. He was about five feet, eight inches tall. He worked at a car dealership in Glens Falls. Ralph had a car and sometimes took the group to Glens Falls.

Elisha Elms showed up one day with his two friends, Dick and Dan Haynes, who were twins. They didn't look alike and Dan was nicknamed "Hulk" because he was so much larger than his brother, Dick. Elisha's older brother, Howard, started coming around too. Howard worked as a farmhand in Hartford. He'd worked there since he was a teen. Howard started making moves on Janette.

Sandra didn't interfere with her mother's life. She didn't believe it was her place to tell her mom what she should do or whom she should marry. It just seemed like it happened so fast. One day Howard wasn't there, and the next day he was.

Sandra woke up early one Sunday morning. It was still dark outside, but she could hear her mother downstairs in the kitchen making breakfast. She got up, and in pajamas, went downstairs to see what was going on. Howard was sitting at the table eating breakfast.

Janette said, "What are you doing up?" surprised to see Sandra up so early.

Sandra replied, "I heard noise in the kitchen and wondered what was going on."

Her mom replied, "I'm just fixing Howard some breakfast and packing a lunch for him. Go back to bed. It's too early for you to be up."

Sandra asked, "What time is it?"

"It's four o'clock."

Sandra went back upstairs to her warm bed. It was November and she didn't want to be up this early in the chilly morning. She remembered now that her mother had told them all the night before that she and Howard had married. Now it made sense. Sandra was still half awake as she heard Howard start the engine of his truck and leave the driveway. She snuggled down under the warm blankets.

On Sundays, Howard only had to work half days because he just had to help milk the cows and feed them. Janette asked Sandra if she would like to go and help. Sandra said yes. Many times she went with Howard in the morning to help. Sandra liked going because she was allowed to feed the calves. They ate out of a bucket of milk that had a rubber teat on it. There were two calves in each stall so she took two buckets at a time and fed the calves. She enjoyed watching them as they attacked the teat by pulling and banging the buckets as they ate excitedly, their tails wagging back and forth frantically as they sucked on the teat.

In the meantime, Howard and Glen Cummings, the owner of the farm, would be milking the cows. Afterwards, the barn cleaner was run and the manure was deposited onto a manure spreader (otherwise known as a honeywagon to those connected with farming), which was attached to a tractor. When it was full, Howard drove it to the fields to spread the manure. He repeated this until the barn was clean. Sandra helped by scraping the manure that had fallen outside the barn cleaner into it with a flat-edged shovel. Sometimes her mom would come to help. Brenda and Gloria would watch Sharon, Michael, and Janet for her.

Frightening Friday

Sandra was bored one summer day and went to visit the elderly couple, Mr. and Mrs. Woods, who lived at the top of the hill nearby. Mrs. Woods invited her in. Sandra liked to listen to stories by older people. They were interesting and they always had some to tell. They became friends and played Scrabble and Crazy 8's. Sometimes Mr. Woods would play a game of Rummy with them.

One Friday afternoon in September, Sandra went to visit with the Woods. The crisp fall air was invigorating. There was no homework on Friday, so she had some time on her hands. The sun would be down soon and she knew that the Sabbath would start at sundown.

Mrs. Woods opened the door when she knocked. "Come on in," she said. Sandra entered the kitchen, closing the door behind her. She watched Mrs. Woods walk over to a chair and hold onto it to steady herself. She was bent over slightly and somewhat bow-legged.

Sandra opened her coat and said appreciatively, "It's nice and warm in here," then sat down as Mrs. Woods motioned for her to take a seat.

"Would you like to play a game of Scrabble?" Mrs. Woods asked.

Sandra's face lit up. "Yes," she answered. Mrs. Woods went to get the game and Sandra went into the dining room where they always played Scrabble.

They set up the game and started playing. Soon the sun dipped below the mountains in the west. Sandra became a little nervous, knowing she should stop playing now that the Sabbath was started. She knew that playing secular games on the Sabbath was prohibited, but decided to finish the game, although she remained uncomfortable. After the game was over and put away, Sandra said, "I better get home now. It's dark out."

Mrs. Woods cautioned her to be careful going home. "Watch out for cars on the road."

Sandra walked briskly down the hill. As she came to a turn, she heard a howl in the distance to the right. Sandra looked in the direction of the howl, then started walking faster. A few seconds later, she heard the howl again, this time a little closer. Sandra started jogging. A third howl, much closer than the other two caused her to run with all her might. She realized that something was coming in her direction and straight toward her. Safety was at home, but the only way there was on this road. On each side of the road was pasture land, bordered by old barbed-wire fences.

As she ran, she suddenly heard an animal running alongside her on the other side of the old fence that enclosed the pasture. Sandra was too terrified to look. The sound of the animal was like that of a dog running through grass. She could hear panting as the animal kept pace with her. Finally, bushes that grew up inside the fenced in pasture stopped the animal from following her. Sandra heard it yelp in pain as it ran into the underbrush in the corner of the pasture.

Sandra sped past the streetlight onto the porch where she tried to catch her breath and calm herself before going into the house. She didn't want to take too long because the porch had no door on it and was afraid the animal might still attack her there. To complicate matters, her mother was pregnant with Howard's baby and she didn't want to frighten her mother by telling her that she'd been chased by some animal that may still be lurking outside their house.

Realizing she was still in danger on the porch, she went inside, trying to be as calm as she could. Her mom noticed the extreme panting and queried, "What have you been doing?" Sandra answered, "Just running home." Sandra often ran, so Janette didn't question further and Sandra didn't offer any more information.

Upon calming down, she got a Bible and started reading it. She prayed, thanking God that the animal hadn't attacked her.

A short time later her mom said, "Dennis isn't home yet. Sandra, go get him at Reynold's house." Sandra put the Bible away.

"Okay," she said.

Sandra put her coat on and, with a prayer in her heart, went outdoors. She paused on the porch before venturing into the yard. She listened, straining to hear anything that might sound like a dog-like animal nearby. Not hearing anything suspicious, she cautiously went into the yard, watching and listening. Her senses were on high alert and she was poised for fight or flight, if need be.

The walk to the Reynold's house never seemed so long. The moon wasn't visible, but it was light enough to see about forty feet around. She arrived at the Reynold's house without mishap. A hearty "come in" answered her knock on the door.

Sandra stepped inside and said, "Dennis, you have to come home now. Mom sent me to get you." Dennis got up, put his coat on, and went with her. They said good night to the family and left.

Now Sandra had to get Dennis home safely without scaring him. Dennis talked as they walked together. Sandra was silent, still in a heightened state of mind. Every sound was heeded. Every movement of grass she could discern was noted. It was with great relief that she opened the door of the house and followed Dennis inside. Before going in, she took one last look to make sure there wasn't anything following them, then quickly entered the house, shut the door, and locked it. Breathing a prayer of thankfulness, she promised to never play secular games during the Sabbath hours again.

Spiritualism

In the *Guides* Sandra received at church, sometimes there would be stories of devil possession of people in other countries, such as Africa. It seemed to Sandra that these things would never affect her in any way.

Soon thereafter, a man was introduced to the family that claimed to be a minister. After a couple of visits, he invited Brenda, Gloria, and Sandra to a youth meeting being held at his church. They had attended many youth functions at the Adventist church and enjoyed them. They all responded that they would like to go.

"What time and when is the next meeting?" Janette asked.

The minister replied, "This Wednesday at seven o'clock.

Janette replied, "I need to get a babysitter for the little kids. I will come with the girls the first time to see how the meetings go."

The minister agreed, "That will be fine. Here's my phone number. Just call me if you will be going." He handed her a card with his phone number on it. After visiting for a short while, he left.

On Wednesday, Janette and the three girls arrived a little after seven o'clock. They went into the church. There were about twenty people inside. They had already started praying. They sat down near the back of the church on the left side of the aisle. Brenda and Gloria had preceded their mother into the pew. Sandra was last coming in behind her mother and sat at the very end of the pew next to the aisle in the middle of the church. The minister excused himself and went up to the front of the church to join the others in praying.

As they watched, a small child fell to the floor. A woman threw a blanket over her. The minister raised his hands and started praying loudly. His hands started to shake. The shaking worked down his arms and into his body. Sandra watched, fascinated, as his body gyrated. Suddenly, her fascination turned to horror as a black teenage girl, violently convulsing, contorted her way down the aisle, straight toward her. She shrank against her mother, attempting to get away from the girl. The girl's eyes were shining and staring. They seemed fixed on something only she could see. After she passed by, Janette said, "Let's get out of here."

Sandra didn't have to be asked twice. She was up and going for the door with Janette, and Brenda and Gloria were right behind her. They left as soon as they could and never returned. Nobody said much of anything on the way back home. The minister was never invited back.

Sandra had an acute encounter with the supernatural forces of evil that night. She made up her mind to never put herself in this kind of position again. She didn't want to give Satan access to her in any way, shape, or form.

Sandra had recognized the workings of Satan from the way the people had acted. Jesus cast demons out of people that were possessed. The people that Jesus cast demons out of were thrown about by the evil spirits, just as these people had been "moved" in unseemly and unnatural movements.

Sandra had read about this kind of possession in the *Guides* from church, as well as the Bible stories of Jesus casting out demons. This was the first time she actually saw someone possessed. She was so glad her mother had gone with them.

Leon

Leon Reynolds and Sandra were only eleven months apart in age. Being a tomboy, Sandra had gravitated towards Leon. He invited her to go tramping through the woods and taught her how to shoot a rifle. Sometimes they would go fishing. Whenever Sandra was bored, she'd look to Leon for company.

One sunny summer day Sandra went down to the creek looking for Leon. Sometimes he went fishing and she liked to be with him. He wasn't in back of his house, so she went to the bottom of Kanes Falls looking for him. The waterfall cascaded about 100 feet down and then the creek continued its winding way toward Fort Anne and the Hudson River. An access road leading to a power plant was located at the base of the falls. Sometimes Leon went fishing below the falls for bullhead.

Sandra walked down the access road humming. As she neared the power plant, she saw a car parked there. A man was sitting in the car on the driver's side. Sandra didn't think too much of it. As she approached from the passenger side, he rolled down the window to speak to her.

"Hi," the man said.

"Hi," Sandra replied. She stopped to talk to him. After all, he was an adult and she had been taught not to be rude to adults.

"What are you doing down here?" he asked.

"I'm looking for my friend," she replied, "Have you seen a boy with dark hair?"

"No," he said. "Was he expecting to meet you here?"

"No, I'm just looking for him."

"Why don't you sit in here with me while you wait for him?" the man suggested.

Sandra looked at the man. He didn't seem to be threatening in any way. She said okay and got into his car. They sat and talked for a while.

"I should be going to look for Leon," Sandra said.

Suddenly, the man grabbed Sandra as she reached for the door handle. "What are you doing?" she cried. She resisted, fighting as hard as she could. Looking up, she spotted Leon walking toward them with his fishing pole and tackle box.

"There's Leon," Sandra said. At that the man looked up and released her when he saw a teenage boy approaching them. Sandra immediately got out of the car. She didn't understand why he had grabbed her or what his intentions had been. Sandra went over to Leon. The man started his car and drove away so fast that the tires kicked up gravel as he went.

"What's going on?" Leon asked.

"He grabbed me. Then when you came, he let me go," Sandra answered. They watched the car disappear up the dirt road.

"Did he hurt you?" Leon asked.

"No." Sandra replied. Then changing the subject she asked, "So, did you catch any fish?"

"Yeah, I got a couple of bullhead," he answered, seeming a little preoccupied.

"So what are you doing down here?" he asked.

"I was looking for you," Sandra said. "I just wanted to talk with you."

A few days later, Sandra was leaning on the bridge by Kanes Falls, looking down into the water as it went under the bridge. It was starting to get dark. Just as she made up her mind to go home, Leon came along.

"What are you looking at?" he queried.

"I was watching the little crayfish in the water before it got too dark," she answered. "I was just heading home because my mother says I have to come inside when it gets dark."

Leon said, "Come down under the bridge. I want to show you something." He started going down the bank next to the bridge. Sandra trusted Leon and followed him under the bridge.

"What is it, Leon?" she asked. It was dark now and hard to see him. The moonlight didn't shine under the bridge. He turned around and came over to her. He started unzipping her blue jeans.

"Leon, what are you doing?" she asked.

"Nevermind," he answered, and continued taking her jeans off. It was so unexpected that she didn't know what was going on. The next thing she knew, she was on the ground and Leon was on top of her. They had wrestled together and been physically close in lots of situations. Sandra didn't feel threatened, but didn't know what was happening.

Suddenly, Leon jumped up and turned his back to Sandra. She got up and pulled her pants on. "What are you doing?" she asked.

"Nothing," Leon said. He wouldn't talk to her and he wouldn't turn around.

"I'm going home," Sandra said and she left.

When she arrived home, she went into the bathroom to urinate. When she pulled her panties down, she saw blood on them.

"I just had my period," she thought. A horrible thought went through her mind. *"What if I get pregnant?"* She wasn't sure what had happened, but somehow related what Leon had done to her with getting pregnant. She prayed, *"God,*

please don't let me get pregnant," then cleaned herself up and went upstairs to bed. After this, Leon seemed to ignore her whenever she was around.

School Standards

Sandra sat fuming in the classroom. She was usually good natured, but sometimes her temper would get out of control. Sandra had met Raymond Martindale and was dating him. Raymond had bought her a watch for Christmas and Mr. Kaiser had taken it away from her.

"You can't wear a ring in class," he said.

"But it's not just a ring," Sandra protested, "It's a watch. You wear a watch. What's the difference if it's on your wrist or on your finger? It's still a watch."

Mr. Kaiser was adamant. "Give me the ring," he said, "Or I'm going to call your mother. You can have it back when you go home tonight."

Sandra didn't want Mr. Kaiser to call her mother. Her mother had enough things to deal with. Sandra didn't want to cause more problems. She angrily handed him the ring and he put it in his desk drawer. When Sandra got in a mood like this, everyone knew her well enough by this time, to just leave her alone and she would eventually get over it.

The word "ain't" was listed on the blackboard as a word that was not to be used. "Ain't, ain't, ain't, ain't, ain't, ain't, ain't, ain't, ain't, ain't, ain't, ain't, ain't, ain't," Sandra blurted out angrily.

Mr. Kaiser was in the middle of giving assignments when he was unceremoniously interrupted by the outburst. The other students just looked down studiously at their books. Some tried to keep from laughing. Mr. Kaiser walked over to the blackboard and gave her three marks.

"You're angry right now, so I'm not going to give you the whole amount of marks," he said.

"Yeah, he knows I'm right. He just won't admit it," Sandra thought to herself.

That afternoon, as school ended for the day, Mr. Kaiser handed the ring to Sandra.

"And don't wear it tomorrow or you won't get it back," he warned. Sandra didn't say anything. She went into Mr. Borgerson's room where the ping-pong table was set up. The others who were waiting for the Fort Anne bus were there, playing "round about." Everyone had a paddle and formed a circle around the table. As they went around, the ball was hit by each individual to the next person in line. The objective of the game was to get down to two players. When one of the two remaining players got *out* determining the winner, another game would start.

Sandra was in a silly mood now. She would get this way when too tired. She made silly remarks and soon had the whole group laughing and holding their sides. Some were laughing so hard they were holding onto the ping-pong table to stand up. Gloria was with the group.

"You're hairless," Gloria gasped.

Sandra looked at her. "What?" she asked, suddenly sober.

Gloria replied, "You're hairless."

Sandra looked quizzical, "I'm hairless?" By repeating what Gloria said she suddenly realized what Gloria meant. "Oh, you mean I'm hilarious!" Sandra cracked up and the rest of the group went into more spasmodic laughter. Someone spotted the bus coming and they all grabbed their coats and ran for the door. They were still laughing as they boarded the bus for home.

Sandra accepted the high standards of the school, but had felt that it was appropriate to wear the ring since it was a watch too. However, the principal didn't agree and made her stop wearing it. Her relationship with Raymond ended not too long afterwards.

Life in the Slow Lane

Living in Upstate New York was like an oasis from the world. The horrible bussing problems of the Southern States didn't touch the people here. The closest thing to the hippie mania sweeping the country was when the hippies came to Woodstock, Vermont to have their week-long rally at a farm. Buses and cars covered with wild paint designs seemed to be endless. Every one was filled with long-haired hippies. For days before the event took place, they could be seen traveling through Fort Anne, Queensbury, Glens Falls, and Hudson Falls on their way to the convocation. Sandra was glad she wasn't part of all that hoopla.

Sandra was aware of movie stars, singers, and entertainers, but her world was so far away from theirs that she never dreamed that she would ever meet any of them. She was aware of the current sensations—Elvis Presley, Ricky Nelson, The Supremes, The Beetles, Doris Day, Rock Hudson, and others, but wasn't really a fan. She enjoyed their music and listened to it on the radio. She watched movies, but didn't buy their records or collect memorabilia.

The one time she did make contact with the entertainment world was when she was ten years old and wrote to the studio where the TV show "Bonanza" was produced. The studio sent her an autographed picture of Lorne Greene, Dan Blocker, Pernell Roberts, and Michael Landon sitting on their horses. However, that photo had been lost when her mother moved after her father's death.

Sandra's family went to the movies and listened to secular music on the radio. They were not convicted that these were not appropriate forms of entertainment.

Sandra was mostly wrapped up in going to church, church school, and church functions. Some people are more apt to be interested in spiritual matters. They want to develop those characteristics that are harmonious with the Bible. It was in this environment that Sandra was most comfortable.

Frank

Brenda and Gloria had left home. They attended Union Springs Academy, a high school run by the Adventist church near Syracuse, New York. Sandra graduated into the big room.

May weather invited her feet to go in search of something to do. School was almost out for the summer. As she walked toward the corner of West Road and South Bay Road, she noticed a new family had moved into the house on the corner. Sandra was friendly and stopped in to meet and greet the family. She walked up to the door and was greeted by a stocky woman coming out with a kitchen rug in her hands to shake out. Sandra stepped aside to let her out and introduced herself as a neighbor that lived up the road in a white house just past the little hill. She gestured with her arm to indicate the direction she lived.

The woman said, "I'm Jennie Campney. Come on in." She was friendly, so Sandra went inside while Jennie talked about the move and where they used to live. Her husband, Arnold, was working on the Gregario hog farm. Her daughter Linda said hi from the bathroom where she was rolling her hair with curlers.

Jennie and Sandra sat down at the kitchen table to talk.

She mostly listened as Jennie told her about some of the places they had lived in Vermont and how Jennie had divorced her first husband and married Arnold.

Jennie talked about her adult children who lived near Fort Anne. Her oldest daughter Dorothy lived at Gregario's farm with her children and husband, who worked on the farm too. Dorothy was pregnant with her fourth child and due to give birth soon. Jim was married and had three children. Joyce was also married and had four children. Frank was in the army and on the way home from the service. He was supposed to arrive any day.

Linda's brother Dennis walked in the house.

"Hi," he said.

"Hi, I'm Sandra."

"I'm Dennis."

Dennis had dark red hair and blue eyes and freckles. He looked a lot like Dennis the Menace from the cartoon strip. He and Sandra hit it off from the start. Dennis invited her out back to see his tree house.

"Okay!" Sandra said. "Show it to me." They went traipsing to the back of the house where Dennis climbed up into a tree. He had some wood and was trying to get it into the tree to make a tree house. There were a couple of boards already laid.

Sandra climbed into the tree with Dennis.

"This is nice," Sandra said and looked around. "We have a good tree to climb in at my house too," she said. "When you come to visit, you can climb it."

"Okay," Dennis replied. They climbed back down.

"I need to go home now. Bye," Sandra said.

"Will you come back sometime?" Dennis asked.

"Sure," she answered. Sandra stuck her head in the door and said good bye to Jennie and Linda. Jennie invited her back whenever she wanted to come. Sandra said okay and went home. She told her mother about the new family that had moved in.

A week later, Sandra was walking by again when she saw a man in an Army uniform sitting on Jennie's porch. He stood up as she approached the porch. Dennis came around the corner and yelped, "Do you wanna play tag?"

"Yeah," Sandra said. "You're *it*," and started running away from Dennis. The man on the porch came down and asked, "Can I play, too?"

"Sure," Sandra said.

He turned around to take the green jacket off. Jennie came out and said, "This is my son, Frank. I told you about him before. Frank, this is Sandra." Frank and Sandra exchanged greetings and then played tag.

The three of them played until they were all out of breath. When they sat on the porch to rest, Jennie came out and offered some lemonade. After they sat and talked for a while, Jennie asked Sandra to join them for lunch.

"What are you having?" Sandra asked. She had learned to ask because she didn't want to eat any biblically unclean foods.

"Hotdogs," Jennie replied.

"Do they have pork in them?" Sandra asked.

Jennie was taken aback by this question then replied, "I don't know. I'll look at the package and see." She went back inside and found the wrapper in the garbage can. Holding the wrapper, she read the ingredients. Looking up at Sandra, she said, "Yes, there's pork in them."

Sandra replied, "Thank you for inviting me, but I don't eat pork."

Jennie had been offended, even though it wasn't Sandra's intention to offend her. Frank listened to the intercourse between his mother and Sandra. He was surprised to hear someone refuse to eat food because it had pork in it. He was intrigued and wanted to know more.

"Why don't you eat pork?" Frank asked.

"Because the Bible says we aren't supposed to eat it," Sandra answered matter-of-factly.

"I never heard that before," Frank said.

"A lot of people haven't heard it before, but that's what it says," Sandra replied. Sandra left when Jennie called Frank in to eat. "See ya later," she said as she left.

Sandra was attracted to Frank. He was tall and good looking. His hair was the color of wet sand. He seemed to be pleasant. Over the next few days, she visited at the Campney residence quite often. A week later, Frank gave her a note to read as she was leaving. She read it on the way home. *"I will love you until the twelfth of never,"* it said. Sandra thought. *"Until the twelfth of never. I wonder what that means."* She ruminated on it for a while. *"It says he loves me. It must mean he will love me forever,"* she finally concluded.

When she visited again just before evening, Frank asked if he could go for a walk with her.

"Yes," she said. They walked toward the bridge by Kanes Falls. Stopping on the bridge, they talked about the note.

"Did you read the note?" Frank asked.

"Yes," Sandra replied.

"What did you think?" he persisted.

"It was very nice," Sandra said.

"I love you," Frank said. Sandra didn't reply. She was starting to feel a little strange.

"Let's go down by the water," Frank said.

"Okay."

They went down the bank to the water's edge. Sandra said, "Look, there are some crayfish and minnows in the water. Do you see them?"

Frank looked and said, "Yes." He walked under the bridge to look around.

He called Sandra over to check out the writing on the wall. She walked over to look at it. Frank grabbed her in his arms and held her. Then he kissed her. As he was kissing her, he stuck his tongue into her mouth. She drew back, disgusted.

"What are you doing?" She protested and pulled away from him. "Let's go," she said, wiping her mouth with her sleeve. As she came out from under the bridge and climbed up the bank, Frank followed.

"I'm sorry," he said.

"Don't do that again," she retorted upset.

The two walked back to Jennie's house. When they came to the driveway, Sandra continued on home without going in. There were some cars in the driveway and kids running around. Sandra waved as she passed by. She didn't feel like visiting anymore.

When Sandra met Frank, he wanted to date her and she wanted to be dated. However, a fifteen-year-old does not understand a lot of things. Frank was six years older than Sandra and this concerned her mother very much.

Frank and Sandra finally became boyfriend and girlfriend. He got a job at the local General Electric plant and bought a white Chevy convertible with a black top. Now he had his own wheels and money so he could invite her to go out.

Whenever Frank invited Sandra to go to a movie or anywhere, her mother insisted that Dennis go with them to chaperone. Dennis wanted one of his friends to go, so usually there were four people for Frank to pay for at the theatre. The Paramount Theatre in Glens Falls was the only place to go to see an indoor movie.

The one place they didn't have Dennis with them was at church. Frank would come by every Saturday and pick Sandra up and take her to church.

Sometimes they would go bowling. Before going to the bowling alley on one of their dates, they went to a department store to spend some extra time with each other. As they walked through the store, they saw some black cowboy shirts with red roses on the front. Frank bought two, one for each of them. When they arrived at the bowling alley, Dennis and Raymond went into the building. Frank and Sandra stayed behind in the car and changed into their new shirts.

"Hurry up, before someone comes," Frank said.

"I'm trying," Sandra replied. "There are too many pins

in it. I don't want to get stuck." After putting them on, they strutted into the bowling alley together. It was exciting trying to get away with something they shouldn't. Sandra knew she should have gone into the bathroom to change her shirt.

Frank and she had been having sex for a short time now. After his family moved to Kingsbury, because his stepfather changed jobs, she had been invited to visit. Frank showed her his room, and in the dark, he started fondling her. One thing led to another and it didn't take long before they were having sex.

Frank was careful not to get her pregnant. Sandra still didn't realize it was sex, but agreed to let him touch her that way. She did know it was something private that she didn't want anyone else to see her doing.

The day came when Frank proposed to Sandra. They were standing in the living room and there were a lot of people around. Suddenly, Frank knelt in front of her and asked her to marry him. She was embarrassed, surprised, and caught off guard, so she just stood there looking at him.

Frank repeated his request, "Will you marry me?"

Sandra was confused, but knew that her church forbade marriage between people of different faiths.

"No, I won't marry you, Sandra said.

Frank stood up. "Why not?" he asked.

"Because the Bible says that people who do not have the same faith are not to marry," Sandra replied. She was firm about it.

One of the things Frank liked about Sandra was that she had very strong religious beliefs. As soon as an evangelistic series came to Glens Falls, he attended the meetings. Frank picked Sandra up and they went together to the meetings. Elder Rainey was the featured speaker. At the end of the series, Frank was baptized and became a member of the Seventh-day Adventist church.

Soon after, he proposed to Sandra again. She looked at him and responded, "No."

Frank asked, "Why not? We have the same faith now."

Sandra hesitated. She knew he wouldn't like what she had to say. "You're too immature," she said.

"What do you mean, I'm too immature?" he demanded.

Sandra thought to herself, *"I knew I shouldn't have told him. Now what do I do?"* She didn't know how to explain to Frank what she needed to say. Her natural instincts told her he was too immature and she had been honest in telling him that. She hoped he would take a look at himself and see where his immaturity was and do something about it. That is what she would have done.

"What do you mean, I'm immature?" Frank asked again.

"Well, in some of the things you do. Some of the ways you act," Sandra replied, avoiding eye contact.

Frank became insistent, "How do you mean?" he asked.

Sandra became silent not knowing how to explain what she needed to say.

Frank muttered, "I'm not immature." Then the subject was changed to her relief. She was not good at conflict at all.

Married at Sixteen

The relationship between Frank and Sandra escalated. Frank still wanted to marry her and she was feeling unhappy at home. Brenda and Gloria were out of the house now, working at Union Springs Academy year round to pay their school bill.

When Sandra told her mother that Frank wanted to marry her, Janette said, "It's easy to get married, but not so easy to get out of it." That was the only advice given to her about the matter. Sandra persisted and her mother finally agreed to sign the papers so she and Frank could get married.

"But you have to be married by Friday," Janette said.

"Okay," Sandra replied. Friday was July 11. Later, Sandra would realize that was her father's birthday.

Sandra called Frank and told him her mother would sign the papers so they could get married. Frank came to pick her up and they went to the town clerk's office to see what needed to be done. The town clerk gave them a list of things to do. They both needed a blood test and Sandra's mom had to come to the town clerk's office to sign the papers.

It was Campmeeting time and the pastor and many of the church members were at Union Springs Academy to attend the yearly convocation. Campmeeting is a spiritual retreat of special speakers and seminars for the church members to attend. It lasts a week. Frank and Sandra called the pastor of the Fort Anne Methodist church. Reverend Van Vleet agreed to talk to them and make arrangements to "tie the knot." Reverend Van Vleet gave them some vows to memorize and agreed to the time on Friday. The ceremony would be held at his house with his wife. Frank's sister Linda and her husband Bob would be their witnesses.

Reverend Van Vleet talked Frank and Sandra into getting rings for the ceremony. Sandra didn't feel comfortable wearing a ring, as she considered it jewelry. But after the Reverend described how the ring symbolizes everlasting love, she reluctantly agreed.

The next day Frank picked her up to go find an apartment in Glens Falls. Janette insisted that Dennis go along with them. Frank and Sandra were amused by it and took Dennis along. After Friday they wouldn't need a chaperone.

Finding a "for rent" sign in a store window, Frank parked the car and they got out to find out about the apartment. The proprietor gave them a key and directions to the furnished one bedroom apartment. After deciding Frank could afford it and it would be close to his work, they went back to the store and made arrangements to rent the apartment.

They stopped at Clarks Department Store to look for some rings. They found some gold plated rings for $3.98 each, which Frank bought for the ceremony. Then they returned to Janette's house and Sandra finished packing her clothes and belongings.

Brenda had given Sandra a pink gown which she had made for a special occasion at Union Springs Academy. It had white lace, which formed a V on the bodice, a full skirt consisting of twenty-two yards of material around the bottom, long sleeves that puffed out at the shoulders, and four-inch cuffs at the wrist that closed with zippers. It was the best Sandra had to wear for the ceremony. She had no money to buy anything else, so it would have to do.

Sandra had never been as emotionally close to her mother as she should have. Brenda and Gloria had always had that privilege. After her father died, she believed she had to fend for herself. Thinking that her mother didn't care about the wedding, Sandra didn't invite her to the ceremony. Frank also had said that his mother wouldn't be there either. Reverend Van Vleet said they only needed two witnesses for the ceremony to be legal.

Friday arrived, bright and beautiful. Frank Bailey drove Sandra to Reverend Van Vleet's house for the ceremony. She was dressed and ready when he came. Bob and Linda were late arriving at Reverend Van Vleet's house, as they had to sneak away from where they were staying because no one else was told about the marriage plans. It was feared that there would be trouble if others who hadn't been invited found out.

The ceremony went off smoothly. Frank drove Sandra back to her mother's house to get her belongings. On the way, he beeped the horn as he drove past the little settlement. Leon cursed as they drove past. Sandra was shocked to hear him, but didn't say anything. Frank acted as if he hadn't heard Leon's cursing. At least, he didn't say anything about it.

Sandra was dressed in the gown, so Frank carried her belongings to the car. Sandra said goodbye to the children and her mother. She felt very awkward and unsure of what to say. Little Howard, who was two years old was very close to Sandra emotionally. She had babysat him most of the time by pushing him in his carriage and taking him for rides. She picked him up and hugged him.

"Bye, Howard," Sandra said. Then Frank and she left for Glens Falls to start their lives together. Upon reaching the apartment, Frank unlocked the door then stood there looking at her.

"Let's go in," he said smirking. He looked at Sandra as if he were doing something funny.

"Aren't you going to carry me over the threshold?" Sandra asked. "It's what you are supposed to do."

"Oh yeah, I guess so," he answered. Frank picked her up and carried her into the apartment.

Once inside, he put her down, then went to get the rest of her things. Frank's clothes were already in the apartment. Sandra sat in a chair and waited for him. After he brought her clothes in, she changed into some jeans and a shirt. They sat and talked for a while before going to bed.

The next morning they talked about a honeymoon. Frank suggested going to his mother's house which was two and a half hours away in Pine Plains, New York. They would use the opportunity to tell them they were married then. On the way there, they decided not to tell Jennie they were married until time to go to bed.

When Jennie told Sandra to sleep in Dennis' room and Frank to sleep on the couch, they protested.

"No, I'm sleeping with Sandra," Frank said smirking.

"You are not!" Jennie ejaculated.

"Yes, I am," Frank responded.

Sandra took Frank's hand. "Come on," she said, leading him toward the stairs.

Jennie started towards them. "You're not sleeping together," she insisted.

Frank and Sandra started laughing. "We were married yesterday," Sandra said. Jennie stopped in her tracks.

"What?" she asked incredulously.

"Didn't you wonder why my brother Dennis wasn't with us?" Sandra asked.

"Now that you mention it, it did seem a little strange that he wasn't with you," Jennie replied.

"Bob and Linda were our witnesses. You can call them if you want to," Frank said. Frank and Sandra held up their left hands to show her their rings.

"Well, I sure am surprised," Jennie said. Then she walked over to Sandra and hugged her.

"Welcome to the family," Jennie said.

This is Marriage?

The first year of marriage was strange. Being sixteen years old and a tomboy, Sandra didn't have much drive to do much. Since it was summer, she had all day to loaf around or do whatever she wanted to. She got a library card at Crandall Library and went there a lot. Zane Grey for westerns and Isaac Asimov for science fiction were her favorites.

Frank worked at a local dress manufacturer as a truck driver delivering dresses to New York City and New Jersey. He went to work every day. Sandra got up to put up his lunches and sometimes make a hot breakfast of pancakes or eggs for him.

On Saturday they attended church sometimes. Sandra had hoped Frank would be the strong spiritual leader of the house, but it didn't happen.

They liked movies and went to them regularly. Frank took Sandra out to the Aust Drive-In Theatre one evening. She didn't realize it, but it was an XXX rated theatre and showed only pornographic movies. Sandra was embarrassed, but had to stay for the whole show because Frank wouldn't leave. Then Frank had her pose nude on the couch with a plastic Santa.

"Spread your legs open," he said. She wanted to crawl

into a hole and hide somewhere, but complied. She felt so degraded and debased.

"Wider," Frank said as he looked through the camera. Sandra opened her knees further.

"Now smile," Frank said. Sandra forced herself to smile then Frank finally took the picture.

"That's enough," Sandra said as she got up to put some clothes on.

"I want some more pictures," Frank protested.

"No, I'm not doing it anymore," Sandra said.

Sandra liked to play Monopoly. She asked Frank to play with her and he didn't want to. He finally said, "If you drink half of this beer, I'll play with you." He had started drinking beer again. Sandra felt very trapped. She didn't want the beer. She hated even the smell of it. All she wanted to do was play Monopoly. Finally, she took the glass and drank the beer, loathing herself for doing it. A couple of times Frank had even hit her.

Sandra gained twenty pounds very quickly. She became discontented after a few months and called her mother. Sandra told her some of the things going on and her mother told her she could leave Frank if she wanted. She could get an annulment, which Janette explained to her.

That night Sandra told Frank she wanted to get an annulment. He started crying. He wouldn't let her tell him what the problem was. He kept saying how bad he felt and that she was at fault for his behavior. Sandra felt sorry for him and dropped the subject. Maybe it was her fault he acted the way he did.

Sandra started her junior year in high school at Glens Falls High. She didn't know anyone and felt totally out of place. The other students were shocked when they found out she was married, which ostracized her from normal teen relationships. By the time November came, she was ready to quit.

Sandra went to the guidance office to find out what she

had to do to quit. She could just write a note, the counselor said, since she was married. She talked to Frank about it first. He didn't try to talk her into staying in school and he had dropped out himself after the eleventh grade. Sandra wrote the note, took it to school the next day, and left.

Sandra soon became bored and tried to find work. She answered an ad at a commercial laundry in South Glens Falls, was hired, and worked three days. When she was told she had to work Saturday, she refused and was terminated.

One evening Mrs. Dow from the church came to visit. She was selling *The Bible Story* books. Sandra insisted on getting a set. Frank agreed to pay for them. This was something Sandra wanted to have in their home, especially when they would have children. The books were familiar to her and she loved reading the stories. It gave her comfort to have them.

In May 1970, there was a knock at the door. When Sandra opened it, a man stood there with a briefcase in his hand.

"I'm a representative of the DeVry Institute of Technology," he said. Frank came to the door and invited him in.

"I sent a card in to this company," Frank explained.

They went into the kitchen to sit at the table. Frank wanted to go to DeVry to be trained in electronics. In the Army he had been a radio mechanic and had liked it. Before the evening was over, Frank had signed up to attend. He was scheduled to start classes in July.

Chicago

Good-byes had been said to all the family. Some of their belongings were stored at Jennie's. The little black Chevy II could only hold so much. It was packed to the brim. Frank and Sandra drove to Chicago.

It took a couple of days to get there. They stopped the first evening in a grocery store parking lot to park and sleep in the car to save money. Sandra couldn't get comfortable, so she pulled out a plastic water mattress and blew it up and put it on the ground next to the car and covered herself with a blanket.

During the night she was awakened by the sound of a car nearby. She opened her eyes to see a police cruiser checking them out. The police didn't bother them, but it made her feel a little safer knowing there were police in the area. In the morning when she woke up, she deflated the mattress and went to put it and her blanket back in the car. When she tried to open the door, she found that Frank had locked it. She was surprised and hurt that he would leave her outside the car and lock the door to protect himself.

Upon arriving in Chicago, the first thing they did was locate the school so Frank could register. At the office Sandra asked about different kinds of employment that might be available in the area. She was told that at seventeen she was too young to work at the manufacturing plants, but she might obtain employment at a local hospital that was nearby.

With directions in hand, Frank drove to the Belmont Community Hospital where Sandra filled out an application for a position as a nurse's aide. She was interviewed and hired immediately. The only thing left to do was to find an apartment to live in that would be close enough to DeVry and the hospital.

Frank and Sandra drove around the neighborhood and found a "for rent" sign in a window. They called the number from a pay phone and arranged to meet the landlord and his wife. It turned out they lived on the other side of the building.

After explaining that Frank would be going to DeVry and Sandra would be working at Belmont Community Hospital, they were accepted as tenants and paid the first month's rent and security deposit. They moved in immediately.

Soon, a routine developed with Frank in school five days a week. He usually drove Sandra to work on her scheduled days then went to school afterwards. On weekends, when they were both free, they would go to the Farm in the Park, the Museum of Natural History, or downtown.

On one such trip they discovered Old Chicago and the Ripley's Believe It or Not Museum. One of the displays was one of Elvis Presley's sequined jumpsuits. They found the original firehouse and Sandra noticed that they were there on the exact day of the 100th anniversary of the fire.

Sandra insisted on finding a Seventh-day Adventist Church and they went one week. It was so hard for Sandra to try to remain faithful to her beliefs when married to someone that really wasn't as interested in it as much as she was. Frank didn't want to go to church and she became tired of trying to explain why she did want to go. She couldn't understand what had gone wrong. She'd done what she believed to be right by insisting that Frank and she have the same faith. Now she had to fight him about religion. It was easier to shut up and stop going to church.

As a nurse's aide, Sandra knew she would have to work on the Sabbath some days, but she also knew that kind of work was a necessity and had to be done every day of the week. Besides, it was the only work available for her at her age.

The work wasn't really hard and Sandra's personality was suited to working with people. She enjoyed talking with the patients and they liked her. Sandra was very conscientious about her work and the head nurse trusted her with setting up the lunch trays when the hospital said the aides would have to be responsible for that.

The day came when Sandra's work tolerance was pushed to the limit. One of the nurses came and told Sandra to come with her. They went to a cupboard where a packet was kept. Then she followed the nurse to a patient's room. There she was shown how to wash, tag, and wrap a dead body.

The hands were placed one on top of the other and tied with soft gauze. A tag with the patient's name was attached to the gauze. Another tag with the name on it was tied to a big toe. Then the body was turned so a wrap could be slipped under and around it, which was pinned with safety pins securing another name tag.

Despite her inward revulsion, Sandra quietly obeyed the nurse and learned what to do for the deceased. Later, she would have to show others how to carry out the procedure, including going down to the morgue and getting the ice-cold gurney to transport the body down there for the mortician to claim it.

When Frank and Sandra had been in Chicago about a year, tension had built up between them. She was tired of working and paying the bills, while Frank only attended school. They were receiving a small subsidy from the G.I. Bill that paid for the costs of DeVry, but that would have to be paid back later.

Sandra wrote a letter to Frank's mother while watching television with him. As she was ready to close the letter, she asked, "Do you want to say anything else to your Mom?"

"Yes," Frank said.

Sandra waited for a few minutes, then closed out the letter, thinking he had changed his mind. Frank finally said he was ready to tell her what he wanted to say.

"I've already closed the letter," Sandra said.

"What did you do that for!?" Frank demanded.

"We can do a P.S.," she replied.

Frank got up, doubled up his fists, and started hitting Sandra. She cowered on the couch and put her left arm and leg up to protect her face and upper body. Frank stopped hitting her and moved away while still yelling at her. Just as quickly as he had started, he had stopped.

Sandra just sat without moving or saying anything. She didn't cry; she just sat and watched television. She didn't answer him either. She didn't realize it, but she was in a state of shock. Then he came over to her and apologized. Sandra looked at him, stunned, unable to say anything. She realized that the love that she once had for him had just died.

The following day at work, Sandra told some of her coworkers what had happened. They told her about serving him with a peace bond. They explained that he would not be able to be near her and would have to move out. They gave her directions to the courthouse and told her what bus to take to get there. On her next day off, she went and made out a complaint.

The officer took her statement and then told her to go sit in the courtroom. The judge called her name and asked what happened. Sandra explained and showed him the bruises on her arm.

"Do you want me to get him out of his class at DeVry?" the judge asked.

"No," Sandra replied

"Okay, I'll send him a letter giving him a court date," the judge said.

"Thank you, your Honor," Sandra said and left.

The next couple of days were strained as she waited for

the letter to come for Frank. He was home on the day it was delivered. He had to sign for it. When he opened it and found out what was in it, he became scared of going to jail.

They talked about what happened and Frank promised he would never hit her again. Sandra agreed to drop the charges against him. She called the courthouse from a pay phone to see what she had to do to drop the charges and was told to not show up for the court date. She told Frank she just wouldn't go. On the court date, Sandra was scheduled to work. Frank was in school. A couple of days later, she received a letter in the mail telling her that the matter had been dropped because she hadn't shown up at the courthouse. Frank then admitted that he had gone to the courthouse on the court date.

Sandra wasn't happy. She wanted to get away from Chicago and Frank. She talked with a co-worker who told her that Sandra could stay with her. Sandra got her address and on her next day off when Frank had school, she packed a two-wheeled buggy with some clothes and walked to her friend's house. She rang the bell and waited for a couple of hours, but her friend never showed up. She found out later that her friend had gone out of town for the weekend. With no place to go, she went back to the apartment.

Frank was there with his friend, Angel, another student at DeVry.

"I've been so worried about you," Frank said.

"Frank really loves you and he has been like a crazy man looking for you all over the city," Angel added.

Sandra was confused, exhausted, and emotionally alone. She started crying and Frank held her on his lap. But there was no comfort in his embrace.

November 1971 finally arrived. Frank graduated third highest in his class. Representatives from companies and firms came to offer him jobs. Sandra wanted to go back to Upstate New York and told Frank that she didn't want to live in Chicago anymore. When he tried to talk her into staying, she said she would go alone and he could stay there. He gave in and said they would go back together. Sandra now weighed 180 pounds. She had gained another twenty pounds while living in Chicago.

Evil Resurfaces

Frank and Sandra packed their car and drove back to New York. The trip was uneventful and they stopped at Jennie's house first. They stayed there a couple of nights. An old family friend, Leon Rivette, was staying with them too. Leon liked to experiment with weird things like "out-of-body" experiences.

After dinner, the family was in the kitchen talking and laughing. Bob and Linda were there with their kids. Sandra had gone into the living room to watch television. She heard some laughing and came out to see what was going on.

Leon was doing some kind of experiment. He would stand behind a person and put his hands on either side of them, then without touching the person, they would fall backwards. Everyone tried to get Sandra to participate in the experiment, but she refused. To her it was along the same line as hypnosis. She had learned that hypnosis was dangerous because it turned the control of a person's mind over to someone else, so she would have nothing to do with it. When Leon approached her, Sandra went around the table and avoided him. The others laughed thinking she was being too straight laced, but Sandra remembered the night that the girl had contorted her way down the aisle towards her and knew that any kind of mesmerizing was of the Devil. She said nothing because they wouldn't believe her anyway. To them it was only a game. Though they laughed and said she was "chicken," Sandra refused to allow Leon to perform his experiment on her.

When Frank and Sandra left a couple days later, they drove north to Hartford, New York, where Sandra's mother lived. The house in Fort Anne had been sold and she now lived in a mobile home on the Cummings farm where Howard worked.

Janette invited them to stay while Frank went into town looking for work. He got a job repairing televisions and radios at Savasta's in Hudson Falls. Paul Savasta owned the business and ran it with his son Peter. Within a few days they located an apartment across the street from Savasta's and moved in.

Daring to Dream

The apartment was small and had no furniture in it. At first, Sandra and Frank used a mattress on the floor to sleep on until they could purchase a bed. Soon they had a table and chairs and living room furniture made of vinyl and metal.

Now that Frank was working, Sandra started looking for a job too. She was hired at a sewing factory, J. & J. Lingerie, as a sewing machine operator. As is typical in the manufacturing industry, there are times when the workload dwindles. One day, a few months later, Sandra's department was sent home before lunch. When Frank came home for lunch, she told him what happened.

"What are you going to do for the rest of the day?" Frank asked.

"I thought I'd go to visit my grandmother for a little while," she said.

Frank went back to work. Sandra lay down on the bed and soon drifted off to sleep. When she awoke, Frank was coming in the door. That evening they decided to go out for a while. Sandra looked for her keys, but couldn't find them.

"Have you seen my keys?" she asked Frank.

Frank went over to the cupboard, opened it, reached up to the top shelf, and handed her her keys.

"What are my keys doing up there?" Sandra demanded.

"I put them up there," Frank replied.

"Why?"

"Because you said you wanted to go visit your grandmother," Frank responded.

"Well, if I can't go visit my grandmother when I want to that's pretty bad!" Sandra screamed at him. "Why don't you just rip up my driver's license too?" she yelled, getting her wallet out and throwing it at him.

Frank looked sheepish. "I don't want to rip up your driver's license," he said picking up her wallet.

"Don't you ever take my keys away from me again!" Sandra said angrily. She was infuriated that Frank would do such a thing. Sandra grabbed her wallet from him. "Just get away from me!" she said disgustedly and went back into the bedroom. Frank left her alone for a while.

Sandra was starting to want more out of life now. It was ridiculous to work every day and have nothing to show for it. She tried to get Frank to save some money. He wanted to have what he wanted now and not be concerned about the future. She did get him to go look at a house that was for sale, but Frank didn't want to buy it. At $20,000, he said it was too much money. Yet when they managed to save up $200, Frank decided that he had to have a stereo that Paul had at the store.

The following summer, Frank's brother Dennis wanted to live with them and look for work. Sandra agreed to let him stay. He slept on a rollaway bed in the living room and Sandra had to edge her way around him to leave for work every day. She was getting more and more frustrated and didn't know what to do about it.

That spring Elvis had his concert via satellite from Hawaii. Sandra watched it on television. At work one day, she wondered what it would be like to meet Elvis. She started daydreaming about it. She imagined how he lived and the kinds of things he did with his friends. She became intrigued by the idea and started fantasizing and mentally living in another world.

The Hawaiian concert was the only one of Elvis's performances that Sandra actually saw. She watched it on television along with millions of other people that day. It was after she saw Elvis in concert when she became determined to change her life. Sandra wasn't sure what it was about the concert that triggered her response; she only knew that it did.

Not knowing how to go about making her life more interesting, she started by imagining what it would be like to meet Elvis and be involved in his life. She soon became immersed in her daydreams. This escape from reality filled all her waking hours. No matter what she was doing, a continuously running story kept going in her head about meeting Elvis and becoming friends with him.

Since Sandra worked as a sewing machine operator, she had lots of time to use her imagination. Sandra was paid by piece rate so the more items she assembled, the more money she made. It would be counterproductive to talk to the other operators while working. As she opened the bundles and laid out the pieces, she would think about going to Memphis and somehow meeting Elvis. When she tired of one story, she started another one.

Sandra believed her fantasy was harmless as long as she wasn't bothering anyone else. Life had become one round of going to work, paying bills, and maintaining an existence. Her escape gave her something to fall back on as she subsisted in a mundane, ordinary life.

In the meantime, Frank was still content to live day by day, without any plans for the future. Dennis never did get a job. Then Sandra discovered that Dennis was taking money out of their little metal box. That was the last straw. Summer was over and Sandra had had enough. After work one day, she told Frank she was leaving.

Still uncomfortable with conflict, she stood in the living

room while he was in the kitchen. She didn't look directly at him.

"I can't live like this any more," Sandra said. "I'm leaving. I trip over Dennis every morning, we don't save any money, we have nothing, and we'll always have nothing."

"Where are you going?" Frank asked.

"I'll find an apartment in Glens Falls," Sandra replied.

The next day Frank drove her to work. They now owned a light blue VW Bug. Sandra assumed he was afraid she would try to take it from him because she had always driven herself to work before. She had no intention of taking the car. Besides, it was in his name. After work, Frank was there to meet her.

"I found you an apartment today," Frank said.

"Didn't you go to work?" Sandra asked.

"I wanted to help you get an apartment," Frank responded. "Come on, I'll show it to you."

Sandra got into the car and he showed her the apartment. It was a nice apartment on a quiet street. Sandra took the number down and called the landlord. It was more expensive than she wanted, but it would do for the time being. It was furnished so she wouldn't have to buy any furniture. The landlord let her move in that weekend.

Fantasy

Sandra really liked the apartment. It was light and comfortable and bigger than the one she had moved out of. She walked to work every day and lost some weight. She had been 190 pounds. She also started going back to church. While with Frank, she had stopped attending because Frank wasn't interested in going any more.

Sandra was still daydreaming about Elvis. Now it was constant. Every waking moment she was living in a fantasy, wishing she could meet him. Although too shy to ever think he might really be interested in her, she lived her life through her dreams.

In her search to make her life better, Sandra read five etiquette books from the library and practiced table manners. She tried to be more aware of her speech and how she sounded to others.

Fall and winter came and went. Sandra met a female co-worker that needed a place to live. Sandra agreed to let her move in if she would pay half of the expenses of the apartment and groceries. The girl agreed.

In Spring 1974, Sandra felt impressed to write to Elvis. She fought it, deciding it wasn't a good idea. Over and over again the thought persisted.

"I wouldn't know what to say," Sandra argued with herself, and dismissed the idea. For about three weeks she refused the idea of writing to Elvis. She didn't understand why the thought persisted. She was afraid to write him, even though she wanted to, because she was intimidated by the thought of his finding out who she was. After all, she wasn't a tall, beautiful model like the other women he was always around.

Then she saw a picture of him on the cover of one of the tabloids. He was smiling with a blonde woman. Sandra couldn't tell exactly what it was about his eyes that drew her, but it seemed as though he was smiling when he really didn't want to. There was something missing in his expression. That made the decision for her. She would write, but wouldn't give her last name or address. That way he couldn't find out who she was. She would try to encourage him with a letter.

Sandra rationalized, *"Why not? He probably gets thousands of letters every week. What's one more? Mine won't be anything special. He's not going to be interested in meeting me just because of a letter."* So she sat down to compose the letter.

"What do I say to someone I don't know?" Sandra asked herself. Then she wrote something like this:

***

Dear Elvis,
My name is Sandie. I hope you are well.

It is still cold and the trees are all bare here. Everything looks gray. I will be glad when the leaves grow again. I like springtime with all the new buds and flowers growing.

I enjoy watching your movies and listening to your music. I hope you are having a nice day.

Your friend,
Sandie

***

She addressed the envelope to: Elvis Presley, Esq., Elvis Presley Boulevard, Memphis, Tennessee and dropped it in a mailbox without a return address.

A couple of weeks went by and Sandra felt impressed to write to Elvis again. It wasn't so hard this time.

***

Dear Elvis,

Just thought I'd write again. I hope you are well. Spring is getting closer. The buds on the trees are starting to come out.

I had an argument with my roommate yesterday. I got so mad I left the house and walked about eight miles. I finally got so tired I had to hitchhike back home.

I have a joke for you. Question: Why are movie stars so cool? Answer: Because they have so many fans. Have a good day.

Your friend,
Sandie

***

About a week later, Sandra wrote again.

Dear Elvis,

I saw the tabloid where a man in England wants to change his name to Elvis Presley. That isn't right. That's your name and you have worked hard to get yourself where you are. You shouldn't let him change his name to yours. I hope you will stop him from changing his name.

Your friend,
Sandie

***

Sandra was dabbling with writing songs. She wanted to meet Elvis eventually and hoped that he would be willing to record her songs. She even paid a company to write the melody for some of her poetry. She got the lead sheets in the mail, but couldn't play an instrument, so she never heard the melody. However, she did get the song copyrighted. In another letter, Sandra asked Elvis if he recorded songs for his friends and told him she was writing some.

As time went by Sandra became bolder in her writing. She told Elvis that she was separated from her husband because he had beaten her three times. She also stated that she did not believe in "one night stands." She didn't want him to think that she wanted to have sex with him because she had low self-esteem. If she ever did get a chance to meet him, she also didn't want to have to worry about him making a move on her, not that he would be interested in her that way anyway.

Sandra sent a Bible verse. «Even the youths shall faint and be weary, and the young men shall utterly fall. But they that wait upon the LORD shall renew their strength; they shall mount up with wings as eagles; they shall run, and not be weary; and they shall walk, and not faint» (Isaiah 40:30-31).

In the same letter, she wrote, «God wants us to meet this summer.» She wrote those words impulsively, not even understanding why she wrote them. She continued writing, «… with most people I have to stop to think, with you I have to think to stop.» Sandra also mentioned that she had told some of her co-workers that she was writing to him. One of the women said that he was like a psychologist for her.

Eventually, Sandra became curious to see if Elvis was actually getting her letters and in a bold move, gave her last name and address. Then she waited to see if she would get an answer. Two weeks went by, then three. No answer came.

"I guess he either didn't get my letters for whatever reason, or he isn't interested in writing to me," she thought.

Sandra wrote more letters telling Elvis he was the greatest performer there was, hoping that would encourage him to write back. Sandra waited, but no answer came.

Sandra felt urged to use her vacation money and time

to take a train to Memphis, but resisted the urge. She was still afraid of contacting Elvis, especially since she had never received a letter, telegram, or note from him.

In the meantime, Frank had lost his job and had come over to cry on her shoulder. He asked if he could stay for the night. Sandra didn't like the idea at all, but tenderhearted as she was, she let him stay. After she went to bed, he tried to get in with her.

"What are you doing?" she demanded. "Get out of my bed."

"I just want to be with you," Frank said. "I love you."

"Go into the other room. And if you try that again you will be out of here," Sandra said. When morning came, she made him leave.

Occasionally there would be free concerts in the evening at the park by Crandall Library. Sandra met some people there and made some friends. One of them was Bob. He was short and had teeth missing in the front, but he was nice. He told her he had seizures sometimes because he had epilepsy.

Sandra became discouraged. She had to move out of her apartment because her roommate wouldn't pay her half of the rent, yet wouldn't leave. The only way Sandra could get her out was to let the apartment go. Sandra moved into a hotel on South Street.

South Street was not Sandra's first choice for a place to live. Her room was three stories over a bar and on weekends the room rocked. It was also more expensive to live there. Work had slowed down too, so she wasn't working every day. It became harder to maintain her room and survive.

Sandra wrote one more letter to Elvis, but didn't give her address because she didn't want him to get the wrong idea about her living in a hotel, especially since she had been very adamant in a letter telling him she didn't believe in "one night stands." Living in a hotel wouldn't look very good.

Living in the hotel was very difficult for Sandra. She had very little food, because most of her money went for the rent.

When Sandra's mother came to get her for the weekends, she ate well then. And one of the ladies she worked with invited her home once a week for a home-cooked meal.

Then one day in April a "Free Concert" sign appeared on the marquee of the Paramount Theatre. Sandra saw the sign and decided to go. It was going to be a religious concert for the benefit of the community.

The day of the concert, Sandra was sitting on the ground in the park with Bob. Bob was lying on the grass stretched out. They were talking and suddenly Bob's body stiffened. She realized that he was having an epileptic seizure, but didn't know what to do. She'd heard that people would swallow their tongue if they stayed on their back, so she rolled him onto his stomach.

Three men came running up to them. One of them grabbed Bob and cradled him in his arms. Then he used a pen to force Bob's mouth open and pressed his tongue down so he wouldn't swallow it. In a few minutes the seizure stopped. The men started to leave.

"Thank you," Sandra said as they left. They didn't answer and kept on going.

"Are you okay, Bob?" Sandra asked.

"Yes, just a little weak. I'll go home now," Bob said.

Bob walked with Sandra as far as the hotel where she lived. Then he went home.

That same night, Sandra went to the concert. When she arrived, it was standing room only. She stood in the middle aisle near the back of the theatre. She could see everything going on from there. Soon a young man came out onto the stage and told his story of how he left his rock band when he became a born-again Christian.

After giving his testimony, he sang some hymns. Then he did an Elvis impersonation with one of Elvis' songs. During the impersonation, he dragged out a part of it and Sandra became bored and restless and started looking around. Suddenly, he ended the song. It was as if he had been signaled to finish because the change was so quick.

At the end of the program he said, "I'm going to pray now. I'm going to kneel, but I know the floor is dirty and I don't expect you to kneel on the floor. Please bow your heads."

Sandra bowed her head reverently. Suddenly there was a pressure on her head and left shoulder and a voice in her ear that whispered, "Kneel, kneel." Sandra knew it had to be her angel touching her and telling her to kneel. Nobody in the crowd was touching her. There was no other explanation and she obeyed.

After the prayer, the young man on the stage was shaking hands with the people. Sandra made her way down to the stage to shake his hand. He shook her hand, then flipped his hand and squeezed hers again in a different way. Sandra made her way to the center aisle to exit the building. She was very happy about the uplifting evening, for the young man who had found Christ, and about feeling the physical presence of her guardian angel.

As she walked, moving along quickly up the center aisle, a man stood halfway up the aisle with a collection plate. Sandra didn't know an offering would be taken and had no money to donate. She felt embarrassed because she didn't have an offering to put into the plate. During this time she was barely subsisting on small cans of fruit and crackers. When Sandra went to church on the Sabbath, she would put all the change she had left from her paycheck into the offering plate there. Sandra had no extra money. She avoided eye contact and started to walk past the man when he addressed her.

"How do you do?" he asked. Sandra didn't' expect the man to address her, and startled, swerved to the right. Then answered to be polite, "Fine, thank you, how are you?" She didn't stop, but instead continued walking up the aisle. She looked up in time to see him turn and look behind him and to his left. He shrugged his shoulders as he looked. Sandra followed his gaze to see a tall man in the shadows standing by the wall.

Then the tall man bent down to speak to another man

on his left. This man immediately started toward the exit to intercept her. Sandra watched as if this was happening to someone else. At the same time he was moving, she kept walking toward the exit. He intercepted her about ten feet from the doorway.

"How do you do?" he asked. Sandra looked at the handsomest man she had ever seen in her life. Puzzled over what was happening, she looked up at him quizzically and replied, "Fine, thank you, how are you?" and she hesitated slightly, waiting for a response. He had the strangest look on his face. He seemed to be surprised by something he saw. For a brief second their eyes met, but he didn't respond back, so she kept on going out the door.

When Sandra stepped outside, she was grateful for the cool April air. She walked to the hotel and went to her room where she got ready for bed, said her prayers, and put on Elvis's "Let's Be Friends" record. While it was playing, she heard the sound of a group of people stop in the hallway. She could hear some men talking in low whispers to each other just outside her door, but couldn't make out what they were saying. After a few minutes of consulting with each other they left.

It was many years later before Sandra understood the implications and the importance of this event. Not only for Elvis, but also the truth in the naïve statement in her letter: "God wants us to meet this summer."

Reconciliation?

In the following weeks, Frank started coming around again hoping to get back together with Sandra. Sandra had given up on ever hearing from Elvis, so she told Frank that she wanted some things to change and Frank agreed. One of her demands was that they have a baby. Sandra had wanted a baby for some time, but Frank would not agree to get her pregnant.

They began having a sexual relationship; however, Sandra remained at the motel because Frank was living with his mother again. After a couple of weeks, she decided she still wasn't happy with him. She made up her mind to tell him the next time he came to see her.

"Frank, I don't want to be with you," she said;

"Why not? What's wrong now?" Frank asked impatiently.

"I don't know. I just don't want to be with you anymore," she answered.

"What if you're pregnant?" Frank asked.

"I'm a big girl now. I can take care of myself," Sandra answered. "I want you to leave now."

Frank left her room. Sandra sat on the bed. *"I wish I had someone to talk to,"* she thought. Sandra got out some writing paper and wrote Elvis a letter. *"I wish Elvis would write back,"* she mused. *"Oh well, this will be the last time I write to him. Evidently he's not interested in writing to me".*

A couple of weeks later, Sandra knew she was pregnant. She told her mother.

"Mom, I think I'm pregnant." Sandra said.

"What makes you think that?" Janette asked.

"I feel kinda sick in the morning and I don't want to eat. But after I eat, I feel better," Sandra replied.

"You better make a doctor's appointment," Janette answered.

"Okay," Sandra agreed.

Janette drove Sandra to her doctor's appointment. Sure enough, she was pregnant. Her due date was February 1975.

The first week of July, the manufacturing plant closed down for vacation. Sandra was still feeling the urge to go to Memphis to meet Elvis, but instead, she went to her mother's for the week. They started talking about living expenses and bills. Janette told Sandra she had a telephone bill of over $100 to pay. Sandra felt that she should help her mother out with the expense, especially since Janette would come and get her for whole weekends, feed her, and take her to church. As much as she really wanted to go to Memphis, helping her mother gave her the excuse she needed to not face her fears. So, she spent the entire week with her mother in the mobile home for her vacation.

Frank started coming around again. Sandra gave in. Her attempt at freedom had failed. Her hopes and dreams of bettering her life crumbled around her feet. But, she still had her imagination. With that she could be surfing in Hawaii with Elvis and his friends, horseback riding, or watching Elvis in concert. What she lacked environmentally, she made up mentally.

Whenever Frank didn't communicate, was unresponsive to her needs, or hurt her in any way, it didn't matter so much any more. She was protected by another life that was beautiful and fulfilling where she wrote songs and movie scripts and was able to enjoy the work of a creative mind. She had intelligent conversations in her imagination. She loved and was loved within her own mind.

Dreams Are Hard to Die

February 17, 1975, Sandra gave birth to a beautiful baby girl, Cassandra. Even while in the hospital, she continued daydreaming and hiding in her secret pavilion.

Sandra and Frank moved to Stillwater, New York and were living in a small apartment there. Sandra had quit her job in November because it was too far to go every day with the bad weather while being pregnant. She was afraid of having an accident. After the baby was born, she didn't go back to work right away.

Two months after Cassandra was born, Sandra wrote to Elvis to close that chapter in her life. She wrote that she had gone back with her husband and that they had a baby girl. She said, "I won't bother you any more."

But still her dreams persisted. She heard about a company that would produce songs written by amateurs and sent for information. When it arrived, she broached the subject with Frank.

"I sent for this information," she said.

"What's it for?" Frank asked.

"It's for people who want to write songs. These people record them and make demos for the writers," Sandra replied.

"We don't have the money for it," Frank said.

"It's $200," Sandra said. "I want to try."

"We don't have $200 to give away to somebody," Frank said.

"What if it works?" Sandra asked. "What if somebody likes my poems? They could be worth a lot of money."

"We don't have the money for you to do it," Frank said.

Sandra put the information away. Would she never be able to do anything she wanted? She was getting frustrated again.

In July one of the radio stations had a month-long special on Elvis. She listened every day as his life was talked about. Again, she felt impressed to try to reach him.

"I must be crazy," Sandra thought. *"He never wrote back. He isn't interested in hearing from me."* But the urge to meet him was so strong. She didn't understand it, but finally decided to attempt to meet Elvis.

Around the third week of August she decided to use the money they'd saved for the rent. With Frank's check on Friday, she would have enough to go to Las Vegas to try to meet Elvis.

That Friday, she started packing things as soon as Frank left the house to go to work. She got out their map of the United States and began plotting her course, when a knock came to the door. She jumped, not expecting anyone to be there. It was her mother. With relief, she opened the door and let her in.

"What's going on?" Janette asked, noting the map spread out on the floor.

"Oh, I just thought I'd go through some things," Sandra replied as she folded up the map lying on the floor.

"Where's the baby?" Janette asked.

"She's in her crib," Sandra replied. They both peeked over the top of the homemade crib Frank had built out of plywood. Cassandra was sleeping peacefully.

"Can I get you a drink?" Sandra asked.

"Sure. What do you have?" her mom asked.

"We have ginger ale, milk, and water. What would you like?"

"I'd like some ginger ale," her mom replied. "Are you sure everything is alright?"

"Yes," Sandra replied as she poured each of them a soda.

They sat in the living room and talked for a while. Sandra invited her mom to stay for lunch and they ate together. Cassandra woke up; Janette fed her a bottle of water, and then said, "I have to go now. The kids will be getting home from school soon."

"I'm glad you stopped by, Mom," Sandra said as she walked her to the door. "See ya later."

Sandra looked at the clock. It was one-thirty. There wasn't much time left. Frank got off from work around three-thirty. Quickly, she put Cassandra in her car seat and drove over to the laundry where Frank worked. She went inside and asked Frank for his check.

"They haven't handed them out yet," Frank said.

"Would you see if you can get it? I need to take care of some things before you get off from work," Sandra said.

Frank got his check and signed it so Sandra could cash it.

"Thank you," Sandra said as Frank handed it to her.

Sandra quickly went back to the apartment and loaded the car. She wrote Frank a note telling him she was leaving and would call later to let him know she and the baby were okay. She drove to the bank and cashed the check.

Sandra drove all of Friday night only stopping to put gas in the car, take care of Cassandra, and make the necessary stops she needed to stretch and eat. She was feeling free and sang hymns as she drove. Saturday morning dawned bright and cheerful. She stopped to feed and change Cassandra. Sandra took her out of the car seat and held her for a while. After a half-hour break, she got back in and drove some more.

By Saturday afternoon she was very tired. She had made it through Pennsylvania and into Ohio. As she traveled on the freeway, she realized she needed to look for a rest stop. She pulled into the parking lot at the next public stop.

Stretching as she got out, she looked around and saw some green grass that beckoned to her. Taking Cassandra out of her seat, she grabbed a blanket and went to the grassy area. Sandra spread the blanket out and lay down in the shade of a tree with Cassandra lying next to her. A little breeze brought fresh air to the weary travelers.

Sandra closed her eyes and rested with her hand on Cassandra's chubby leg. She didn't want to go to sleep and take the chance that someone might grab her.

A few minutes later, Sandra heard a woman talking near her. She opened her eyes and found a man and a woman standing close by, presumably talking about Cassandra. When Sandra sat up, the woman addressed her.

"Hi. We were just noticing your baby. Are you traveling alone?" the woman asked.

"Yes," Sandra replied.

"Where are you going?" the woman asked.

"I'm going to Las Vegas," Sandra replied.

"What will you do there?" the woman asked.

"I will get a job and work. I can work at a restaurant or a hotel," Sandra answered. The answers came quickly to her. She hadn't really thought about what she would do when she reached Las Vegas. She didn't even know anything about Las Vegas, except Elvis probably went there a lot.

"My husband and I want to give you a little something to help you," the woman said.

"Oh, I have money," Sandra responded. She felt uncomfortable with taking money from people she didn't know.

"Well, take it for the baby then, the woman said, then nudged her husband to give Sandra some money for the baby. The man took out his wallet and leafed through the bills in it. Sandra glanced at the wallet unconsciously. When she looked up the woman was smiling at her. Sandra blushed with embarrassment. The man handed his wife a twenty-dollar bill, which she handed to Sandra.

"Thank you," Sandra said awkwardly as she accepted the money from her. "Where do you live?" Sandra asked the woman.

"We live in a suburb of Chicago," she answered.

"I used to live in Chicago," Sandra said.

"Good luck," the woman said as she and her husband started walking away.

"Thank you," Sandra said. She watched as the couple walked to their car and got in. They waved and Sandra waved back as they drove away. Then she sat down on the blanket for a few more minutes.

"Well, we might as well get going," Sandra said to Cassandra, "I guess I'm rested up now." She picked up the baby and the blanket and went back to the car.

That night, exhausted, Sandra ran into some roadwork. She seemed to be going around in circles as she drove. Finally, she stopped, locked the doors, and tried to get some sleep near some trucks pulled over on the side of the road. She felt safer near the truckers than if she had stopped in an isolated area.

After a restless night's sleep she woke to a cooler day. She took care of Cassandra and then started out to find a restaurant or gas station where she could get some hot water to make warm cereal for the baby.

The roadwork had detoured Sandra from her route and she found herself in a rural farming area. Finally, she spotted a store and stopped to rest and fix a bottle for Cassandra. When she came out of the store, a car had stopped and was looking at a sign about a dance going on that night.

"What's this shindig all about?" a woman asked her.

Sandra answered, "I don't know, I'm just passing through."

Someone in the car asked, "What'd she say?"

The woman answered, "She doesn't know. She's just passin' through."

Sandra watched as they drove away. *"I'm just passin' through,"* she thought. It sounded like a line from a movie.

Sandra started thinking that Frank was probably worried about them. She didn't like taking Cassandra away from him. After all, he was her father. Now guilt started setting in. Sandra put Cassandra in her car seat and got back in the car. Cassandra drank from her bottle as Sandra drove into the west.

As Sandra drove, she started thinking about going to Las Vegas. She was all by herself with a baby. What kind of a job would she get? How would she provide daycare? What would Elvis think? She was a married woman trying to meet Elvis Presley. And, she had written that she would never bother him again. What would he think of her, especially with a baby? What would other people think of her?

That night she stopped to call Frank. She was feeling guilty for leaving the way she did. *"If he yells at me, I'm going to hang up and keep on going,"* Sandra said to herself. It was around eleven o'clock in New York when she called.

"Hello," Frank answered.

"Hello. This is Sandra."

"Where are you and what are you doing?!" Frank yelled into the phone.

"I'm in Ohio," Sandra answered.

"What are you doing in Ohio?" Frank demanded.

"I'm not happy anymore," Sandra answered. She started feeling even guiltier now that she had called.

"You can't take Cassandra away like that," Frank said. "You can be arrested. Cassandra's my daughter too."

"I don't know what to do," Sandra said.

"Come back here and we'll talk about it," Frank said a little more calmly.

"All right, I'll come back," Sandra responded. "Goodbye."

Sandra got into the car, turned it around, and headed east. She was no longer happy and hopeful as she had been when traveling west. She started indulging in her fantasies again. The thought of going back to her husband, even though that life was all she knew, was uncomfortable. She began fantasizing again to comfort herself. She had promised to return and that was what she did. Darkness settled upon her mind as she indulged her fantasies and allowed herself to fall back into the despair of hopelessness.

Sandra arrived in Stillwater late Monday night. Frank was sleeping when she arrived. He woke up as she came into the apartment. After putting Cassandra to bed, they went to bed too. Frank didn't want to talk because it was too late, but he insisted on having sex.

Working, Wishing & Weeping

After Frank came home from work Tuesday, they talked about moving. Sandra wanted to go back to work. Frank would quit his job at the laundry and they'd move back to Glens Falls where he'd get another job. She called the manager of J. & J. Lingerie on Wednesday and was hired back. They were moved by the end of the following week.

In December Sandra told Frank she wanted another child so Cassandra wouldn't be raised alone. "It would be best if she has someone to play with as she grows up," Sandra said. Frank didn't really want any more children, but he agreed to keep her happy.

Maybe it was because Sandra knew she was going to get pregnant, or maybe it was just a special time for her, but whatever the reason, that night she experienced the best sex she'd ever had.

The following September, Sandra gave birth to another daughter. Frank had chosen Cassandra's name, so they agreed that Sandra would choose this baby's name. She went to the Bible to find a name for the baby and decided on Priscilla. She was born September 5, 1976. She had red hair and light blue eyes. Sandra called her "my bicentennial baby" because she was red, white, and blueand because she was born in the bicentennial year of the United States.

Sandra still kept on having fantasies about Elvis. Even now, she hadn't put two and two together and realized that Elvis had been in Glens Falls two years earlier to meet her. Yet the urge to write to him kept coming back to her. At Christmas she felt impressed to send him a Christmas card, but believing he was not interested in hearing from her, quelled the impulse and didn't do it.

When Elvis's birthday came, she was again impressed to send him a card and wish him a happy birthday. Again, she didn't do it. Spring came and Elvis was in the hospital. Sandra felt compelled to get a card. She actually bought one, but then didn't send it, still believing Elvis would not want to hear from her.

The next summer a contest for religious songs was announced over the radio. Sandra made up some lyrics, but then didn't send them in. What was the use? Frank wouldn't support her and let her try. She didn't know how to write the musical score and she wouldn't be allowed to use money to get a melody for it. Frank expected her to keep her mouth shut and not have any dreams of her own. As long as she did that, there was peace in the house.

The morning of August 16, 1977, Sandra woke to the radio alarm clock. As she lay in bed daydreaming about boarding Elvis's plane in Las Vegas, the news came on that Elvis had died earlier that morning. Her eyes opened and she listened intently. It couldn't be true. Elvis couldn't be dead.

Sandra got out of bed to get ready for work. The announcement came again. Elvis had died. She sat on the bed in shock. Then the children demanded attention. Sandra dressed for work. Jennie came to watch the girls. Sandra was paying Jennie $35 a week to watch them so she could work. Sandra got her money's worth. Jennie also cleaned the house for her and even prepared some meals.

At work everyone was talking about Elvis. Sandra said

nothing. She went to her sewing machine and just worked. The day seemed interminably long. To keep from acknowledging the loss, she engaged her mind in fantasies. Not current ones, but predated to when Elvis was living.

The next day Sandra woke up sick and had to call off from work. Then she called Jennie to tell her not to come to watch the kids. Sandra couldn't afford to pay Jennie if she wasn't working since she had no sick-time benefits at that job. She watched the two girls herself. Sandra was sick the rest of the week with bronchitis.

The day of Elvis's funeral, Sandra watched as his coffin was carried out of his house and taken away. She cried and cried lying on the couch with a towel for her face and a bucket to expectorate into. With the bronchitis and the emotional loss, Sandra was a mess. It was actually a blessing to be home for that week, where she could mourn without having to explain what was wrong with her. The children were too young to ask questions or understand.

Just as she had been given time when her father died to be away from the rest of the family, she now had time to grieve for Elvis and she allowed herself to do so. God was still holding her in the palm of His hands.

Other Dreams

That fall, Frank and Sandra contacted the Seventh-day Adventist school board about a piece of donated land it had up for sale. The property was halfway between Fort Anne and Hudson Falls on Route 4, a major highway with many trucks traveling through on their way to and from Vermont.

Frank and Sandra had to appear before the school board to request buying it. Fortunately, their request was approved and they were eager to start building. However, because a farmer had been renting the property to grow corn, they had to wait until after the harvest and didn't start building until the following year.

Frank had a four-wheel drive Chevy Blazer, which was helpful because there were no roads to the property, which consisted of rough pasture land with rolling hills and a stream at the base of a hill. Frank built a makeshift bridge to cross the stream, enabling him to drive all the way to the property. Because she couldn't drive her car on the clay soil when it was wet, Sandra had to park her car by the main road and walk to it.

That summer they hauled boards and other materials up to the site and built a 24'-by-24' house on cement blocks. Tar paper was used to cover the roof and walls to waterproof them. Although they had no running water or electricity, Frank and Sandra moved into the home that July.

Frank had to leave for his two weeks of National Guard training in Glens Falls. Sandra would get the girls up every day, walk them out to her car, and take them to Jennie's house. From there, Sandra went to work at the Joy Department Store. After working there, she went to the Sheraton Inn, where she worked as a maid until eleven o'clock at night. Then she would go get her sleeping girls and drive home. She would carry Priscilla while Cassandra walked beside her in the dark all the way up to the house.

Often Sandra recalled the time she was chased by a wild animal in the dark when she was a child and she prayed for protection. There would have been no way to outrun an animal while walking to her property, especially with two small children. Aside from having gained a lot of weight, the slippery clay ground would make running impossible. Her prayers were answered and nothing happened.

Because the house was built on blocks and there was space between the floor boards, wild animals could get into the house. Sandra had been awakened a couple of times by the scratching of one making its way in. She would get up and stomp on the floor to scare it away. After the noise would stop, she'd go back to bed.

One time when the scratching started again, Sandra quietly got out of bed, grabbed a broom, and stood by the wall waiting patiently for the animal, a skunk, to come in. Sandra sideswiped the animal against the wall, forcing it to fall back down under the house and convincing it to leave. It didn't come back again.

The night maid job was temporary and would end after the races were over at the Saratoga racetrack. During her stint there, the Doobie Brothers stayed while performing at the Saratoga Performing Arts Center (SPAC). Sandra got permission from her manager to go into the bar and get an autograph from Pat Simmons and some of the others.

Impressed with Mr. Simmon's signature she told him, "You have better handwriting than I do. Thank you for the autograph."

Finances were so tight that Frank and Sandra didn't have enough money to get cough syrup when Priscilla got sick. At that time a salesman stayed at the Sheraton for a couple of days. One evening he asked Sandra if she would be interested in making some money. She asked how and he suggested having sex with her. Sandra thought, *"I need to get some cough medicine for Priscilla,"* so agreed to go to his room after she was done working.

After clocking out, Sandra got into her car and drove down the driveway as if leaving for the night. At the end of the road, she turned around and drove back to the hotel to the man's room and parked outside. He let her in through the glass door. She had gotten permission to shower earlier from the night manager in one of the empty rooms.

The first thing she asked was, "Do you have any protection?"

He answered, "Yes."

Sandra said, "Okay."

When it was over, she told him that she couldn't stay because she lived with her mother who would be expecting her home. She took the money and quickly and quietly left. Sandra didn't want him to know she was committing adultery. She felt bad enough about what she was doing. He didn't have to know too.

On the way home Sandra stopped at the grocery store to buy cough syrup, which she gave to Priscilla when she got home. When Sandra finally crawled into bed, Frank wanted sex too. At this point she didn't care. It just didn't matter anymore. Sandra was pleased to hear Priscilla breathing easier as she fell asleep.

The family lived in the house until late September. It became so cold they couldn't keep it heated, even with the kerosene stove they had bought at Sears. They finally moved out into a motel room in South Glens Falls.

Tough Times

Living in the motel wasn't so bad. Bob and Linda lent Frank and Sandra a propane camp stove. The room came with a refrigerator so keeping groceries on hand was no problem. They weren't sure the owners would approve a stove in the room, so they kept it covered up with material and used it as a shelf when not cooking.

Frank was working as a maintenance man at a trailer park and Sandra was still working at the Joy Department Store while Jennie babysat during the day.

Frank decided to go back into the Army to put in enough time to later retire. He re-enlisted and was shipped out to Fort Dix, New Jersey at the end of January 1979.

After her job ended at the Joy Department Store after the Christmas Season, Sandra received unemployment compensation that was just about enough to cover the room's rent. She also applied and received food stamps after Frank went into the military. Frank would not get paid until the end of the first complete month that he was in basic training. Sandra found a way to supplement her income by selling Tupperware for a few months.

Between looking for work to remain eligible for unemployment and doing Tupperware parties, the car broke down. Sandra was now without transportation and the motel was located a good five miles outside the town of Glens Falls. In desperation, she called Jennie to see if Arnold could take a look at the car. Arnold was not a mechanic, but he was able to fix it by replacing the starter.

One of the bill collectors even came to the motel to claim the cleaning products they had purchased. "They're in our house a quarter mile off the road. If you want to walk through the snow and go get them, be my guest. Here's the key," Sandra held the key out to him. He just looked at her and said, "Do your best to send us a payment when you can," and then he left.

The stress of taking care of the children and having little money, food, and resources took a toll on Sandra. Frank's eight weeks of basic training ended around the last of March. He would be graduating and he wanted Sandra and the girls to come to Fort Dix. Sandra packed up some clothes and food, choosing to drive to Fort Dix at night because the children would sleep all the way there. They finally arrived early Saturday morning. After being admitted on the base with her military ID card, Sandra drove around looking for Frank. With several ranks of soldiers moving around on the parade field, she couldn't tell which platoon Frank was in. It was impossible with all the men wearing matching uniforms.

Driving slowly along the road, she saw a soldier running towards and hailing her to stop. It was Frank. He got in the car and directed her to the barracks where he had been staying. Cassandra and Priscilla were happy to see their daddy and gave him hugs and kisses.

Sandra was exhausted and wanted to get to a motel so she could lie down and get some rest after driving all night. Before leaving the barracks, Frank introduced Sandra to his drill sergeant. The drill sergeant had previously given Frank encouragement when Sandra had told him she wanted to separate again.

Sandra was tired and not ready to meet anyone, but Frank

insisted. He was proud of his accomplishment in getting through basic training at the age of thirty-one. When he had first shown up with the other recruits, the drill sergeant had given him a hard time because of his age and had tried to "break" him during basic training, but Frank was healthy and in better shape than most of the eighteen-year-old enlistees. Frank was able to do more push ups and run farther because he didn't smoke or drink. He had earned the respect of his drill sergeant and deserved the recognition, so Sandra agreed to be introduced.

In spite of her appearance, being overweight and exhausted, the drill sergeant was polite and courteous. Sandra could tell from his expression that he was surprised to see how heavy she was and probably wondered why Frank was so enamored with her. Then they left to get a motel room for the weekend.

There was a motel within a few miles of Fort Dix and they rented a room. Frank sent Cassandra and Priscilla outside to play so he and Sandra could have sex. Sandra protested to no avail. She wanted to wait until evening and enjoy the sex without worrying if the girls were all right. Frank was insistent, so she let him have the sex he wanted. It didn't take long as he hadn't had any since starting basic training two months before.

Sandra got up as soon as it was over and checked on the girls. Since it also happened to be Frank's birthday, he wanted to go to the ocean. The family drove down to the beach. It was cold and windy and the waves were rough and high. Cassandra and Priscilla enjoyed running away from the water as the tide came in, squealing and making tracks in the sand. They collected some small shells to take back to the car. Frank jumped into the water and came out a lot faster than he went in. Then he dragged Sandra over to the water and threw her in. The water was so cold that Sandra couldn't catch her breath or move so Frank had to go in to pull her out.

They wrapped towels around themselves and went back to

the car. The girls had gotten wet but weren't totally soaked like their parents. Once in the car, the sun warmed them up. They found a restaurant, ate lunch, and then returned to the motel room. Frank took Cassandra and Priscilla outside and played with them so Sandra could finally get a little rest.

Frank had a weekend pass and had to return to the barracks on Sunday afternoon. Before he could go home with his family, he had to finish some final paperwork and get the orders for his next assignment. Sandra dropped him off and then left to drive back to New York. A few days later Frank came home on the Greyhound bus.

Fort Hood & Rebirth

Frank had thirty days to pack, get a decent car, and report to his assignment for the next year in Fort Hood, Texas. The family bought a yellow Buick to make the Texas trip and all they took with them were clothes and household items that would fit into the trunk.

Sandra helped plan the driving route to Texas and found a way to go through Memphis, Tennessee on the way. Although not stopping there to see anything, it gave her some comfort to know they would be on the freeway near Elvis' house. She still used her "make-believe" world to cope with the unpleasant realities of her life and situation.

Frank and Sandra took turns driving the car so they wouldn't have to stop much along the way. The trip was uneventful and they arrived in Fort Hood early one morning. After locating the army base, they snoozed in the car until business hours began. Frank got directions to his company and reported to the office of his unit.

Now they needed to find a place to live. They bought a local newspaper and found an agency listing apartments and houses for rent. The agent had a two-bedroom house for a reasonable rent. He gave them directions and met them there. They took it immediately.

The house was about twenty-four feet by twenty-four feet sitting up on blocks. It was light and airy and on a quiet dead-end street. The house was furnished with beds, a couch and chair in the living room, and a small dinette set in the kitchen. Behind the house was an apartment building. The next-door neighbors were African-American on both sides, which didn't bother Sandra, but she hadn't ever interacted with people of other races, except for a few visitors in church. Sometimes, when driving through Albany, New York, she had seen African-Americans sitting on their steps outside their apartments, but she hadn't had an actual speaking relationship with any. All that would change while living there.

After signing the lease, Frank and Sandra carried their belongings into the house while the children played outside. They then went grocery shopping. Upon returning, Sandra cooked a meal. That evening everybody settled down into the new living quarters quickly.

Frank had a couple of days off before having to report for duty, so the family drove around town to check out their surroundings. They located the library, Laundromat, and local stores for future reference. They drove on base to locate the store and other facilities that were available for military families.

The neighbor children came over to play with Cassandra and Priscilla. A swing hung from a tree on the other side of the road directly across from the house. Frank and Sandra sat on the porch and watched. The kids all seemed to get along all right. The mother of the other children came out and told her kids they had to come in for dinner. Sandra took the opportunity to introduce herself. The woman responded by coming over to the fence and shaking hands with them.

After a few weeks, Sandra decided to start going to church again. They had fallen away from regular attendance and she missed it. She looked up the address in a phone book at the Laundromat and then asked for directions on how to get there. She made up her mind to go the next Sabbath.

On Sabbath morning, the girls and Frank watched cartoons after breakfast. Sandra put the dishes in the sink, went to the bedroom, and changed into a dress for church. When she came out, Frank was surprised.

"Where are you going?" he asked.

"I found a Seventh-day Adventist church and I'm going to go," Sandra replied. "Do you want to come with me?"

"No," Frank said.

Sandra looked at Cassandra and Priscilla and asked, "Do you want to come to church with Mommy?"

"No," they answered in unison with their eyes still fixed on the television screen.

"Okay, I'll see you later," Sandra said and left the house. She knew after a couple of weeks they would go, if only to see where she went and what she did. It felt good to go again.

The service was interesting and was similar to what Sandra was used to. The pastor was young with a wife and two small children. They invited her to come back again next week and Sandra made up her mind to do that.

After going home, changing her clothes, and eating lunch, the family went swimming at a local lake that had a playground for the kids. After sunset they walked around in some stores for something to do.

Just as she thought, a couple of weeks later, when Sandra was getting ready for church, Priscilla said she wanted to go. Sandra asked Frank and Cassandra if they wanted to go and they said they did too. The girls really enjoyed the Sabbath School with the songs, fingerplays, and stories and were happy that they had come. For the rest of the time that the family was stationed at Fort Hood, Cassandra and Priscilla went to church with her every week.

One Sabbath morning, when Sandra asked Frank if he wanted to go, he replied, "No, church is boring," right in front of the girls. Sandra gave him an upset look, and after putting the girls into the car, went back inside and told him not to say that in front of them. He defended himself and said that church was boring again. Sandra said that it wasn't boring to her and left him to watch his cartoons.

Frank did attend church occasionally until he made friends with Jan and Ken Jones. After that he went more often.

After being a church member all her life, Sandra was now beginning to understand how it all made sense. She read a book entitled *The Desire of Ages* by Ellen White about Jesus' life on Earth. Sandra was having a spiritual awakening and was impressed to make positive changes in her life and behavior.

Sandra was still having fantasies about Elvis even though he was dead. She was convicted that these fantasies were wrong and started fighting the thoughts when they came into her head. She made deliberate choices to keep from letting her thoughts go in that direction. Then she felt that she should give up eating ice cream. When she told Frank, he made fun of her saying, "A little ice cream won't keep you out of Heaven."

Sandra appealed to Jan and told her what Frank had said about her decision not to eat ice cream any more. Jan told Frank to leave her alone and that it was Sandra's choice to make if she didn't want to eat it. Frank scoffed again at the idea of giving up ice cream.

Then Frank went away for two weeks for desert training at Fort Irwin, California. While he was away, Sandra read the story of Jesus in the Garden of Gethsemane in *The Desire of Ages*. It described the awful agony Jesus suffered and how great drops of blood formed on His brow and caused Him to almost die before even being crucified. A sense of the pain and price that Jesus paid overwhelmed Sandra as she lay in her bed contemplating the cost of her salvation.

In a burst of thankfulness and wonder, she started praising God and Jesus for the sacrifice They had made for her so she would be able to go to heaven. Her praising was done mentally so as not to wake up the girls who were sleeping in their room. Suddenly, she was transported in mind to the base of the great white throne in Heaven. She was bowing, worshipping in truth and beauty and holiness before God Himself. Wrapped up in the love of God's gift of eternal life through Jesus, she continued praising soundlessly with perfect love and praise.

As she knelt in adoration, she could feel the angels pass by her on the right-hand side as they ascended and descended the steps. Even though her eyes were closed, Sandra was aware of a great bright light all around her. Lost in her praising, she could feel the absolute acceptance that was bestowed upon her. It was as if she was not only welcome there, but that she belonged.

Abruptly the bed shook and Sandra heard the sound of something or someone hitting the footboard of the bed. Her concentration broken, she detached from the wonderful experience. Sandra opened her eyes, but there was nothing there to hit the bed and nobody was in the room. She realized that either Satan or one of the fallen angels had had to leave her room because she had been in the presence of God and they can not be in His holy presence. With malice and resentment, the evil presence had protested by kicking her bed on the way out of the room.

Filled with wonder and awe, Sandra wanted to tell somebody what had just happened. She got out of bed, called a young couple that belonged to her church, and asked if she could come over for a few minutes. They seemed to be hesitant, but she was so excited, she insisted that she had to come and tell them something. They finally said she could.

Sandra got the girls out of bed and carried them to the car. They were still sleeping. She didn't dress them and let them continue to sleep. When she arrived at the couple's home, she quickly told them what had happened to her and then realized that the two had been arguing about something. They didn't respond to her story so she left and went home.

Sandra was still enraptured with the experience and wanted to share it with someone, but there wasn't anyone to tell. She put the girls back into bed and went to bed herself. Before going to sleep she decided not to tell anyone else what had happened.

"*Nobody will believe me anyway,*" she thought. "*And Frank will only make fun of me if I tell him.*" Sandra fell asleep so peacefully that night.

Sandra Bailey, 1973

God's Gifts

One hot night, Sandra left the front door open with only the screen door shut. The windows were open to catch any breeze that might pass through.

In the morning, Alice, a friend who lived in the apartment building in back of the house, asked if Sandra had been bothered by the drunken soldiers that had come through their road during the night. They had been going door to door trying to open doors, yelling and making noise. Sandra said she hadn't heard anything. She and the girls slept through the night without any disturbance at all. But after that, she locked the front door no matter how hot it was. They had been protected from harm by the angels and Sandra knew she needed to protect herself as well as she could from then on. To not protect herself and the children would presume that God would take care of her even if she were careless—and she knew better than that.

In church, a young mother's name and address was given out who needed some food. After lunch, Sandra went through her cupboards to make up a care package for the young girl. Alice came over to visit while she was making up the box.

"What are you doing?" Alice asked.

Sandra told her about the young mother as she continued

filling the box. Alice commented that Sandra didn't have very much food herself, asking if should she be giving away the little she had to someone else.

"God will take care of us. He always has and He always will," Sandra replied.

Sandra invited Alice to come with her. They found a girl sitting on the porch holding a little baby.

Sandra introduced herself and asked the girl if she was the person named on her slip of paper. The girl said she was, so Sandra explained that the girl's name had been given out at church and that they had come to give her a box of food to help her out. Sandra and Alice stayed and visited a while before going home. Alice still thought Sandra should not have given her food away.

On Monday Alice came by to visit again. While she was there, the mailman came. Sandra got a letter from Jennie and inside it, totally unexpectedly, was a money order for ten dollars. When Frank and Sandra had left Glens Falls, Jennie had agreed to buy their old car from them. Jennie sent money whenever she could. They never knew when it would come. Sandra held up the money order for Alice to see.

"You see, God takes care of us," she said. "Now I can replace the food I gave away." Alice was surprised.

A few days later, Frank returned from Fort Irwin and life resumed its normal course. Sandra reveled in her new-found faith and kept her secret. Frank kept saying things that hurt and discouraged her. Sandra tried so hard to keep from slipping back into the old habit of fantasizing when hurt, but eventually she started doing it again. As she regressed back into her "escape," she could literally feel the Holy Spirit withdraw from her. But living in the real world was too painful.

The year at Fort Hood went by fast. Frank was issued orders to go to Germany for his next assignment. He was given a month off to get ready to go. It didn't take long to contact all the utilities to get a shut off date and let the rental agency know they would be moving. The floor had become very badly scraped up, so Frank bought some gray paint and painted it to get the deposit back.

With the car loaded up and the girls settled in, they started their trip back to New York where Sandra would stay with the girls until orders were cut for her to live in Germany. It would take some time for quarters to become available. Until that time, they would have to stay stateside. Frank and Sandra decided it would be better if she lived near the family in case of an emergency

While Sandra was driving in the middle of the night, Priscilla woke up. She pulled herself up close to the back of Sandra's seat and started singing "Jesus Loves Me." Sandra felt the holy presence of God fill the car and she knew He was still with her even though she was sinning.

They arrived in Glens Falls about 10 p.m. They drove to Jennie and Arnold's, who had agreed to let them stay with them temporarily. Arnold now worked for Burns Security Agency and they lived in an apartment complex in town. The regulations there allowed visitors for a short time only, so they got the okay from Janette to stay with her for a few nights too.

The month went by quickly. By the time Frank left, Sandra was set up in the basement of Jennie's apartment with a bed and a few chairs. It was big enough for her and the girls temporarily.

After a few weeks of living there, Sandra knew she had to get a place of her own. It wasn't working out at Jennie's. Conflicts arose concerning Jennie's kitten. Jennie didn't want the girls, who like most children love to play with baby animals, touching it. Sandra searched the newspaper to find another place to live and located a mobile home for rent in a rural area of Fort Anne. She moved in as quickly as she could and stayed there until time to move to Germany.

Sandra had to go into town to do the laundry, as there were no laundry facilities in the mobile home. On one such trip, she had just enough money to do the wash. Cassandra was in kindergarten and she needed clean clothes to wear to school. Sandra had no more money for gas or food until Frank's check would come at the end of the month. She had enough gas to get home, but probably not enough to get back into town. She wondered how she was going to get by.

Sandra crocheted while watching the girls play in the Laundromat. As she wondered what to do, a voice whispered to her, "Go outside and walk around." Sandra stopped crocheting for a moment then started again. "Go outside and walk around," the voice said more emphatically. Sandra put her crocheting away.

"Come on kids, let's go outside for a little while," she said.

Cassandra and Priscilla joyfully went outdoors with her. Sandra put her crochet bag into the car and they all walked towards the back of the Laundromat. Still preoccupied, she meandered along with the girls. Then something lying on the ground caught her eye. Sandra went over and picked it up. Unfolding it, she discovered a twenty dollar bill! There was no doubt it was a gift from God. Sandra thanked God for His providence while walking with the girls until the wash was done. She put the tithe aside, bought some groceries, and put gas in the car. There was just enough money to hold them over until the next check came from the military. God had come through for her again.

In October Frank received orders for Sandra and the girls to come to Germany. Temporary housing had opened and they could go. The military contacted Sandra to move her belongings.

With fear and trepidation in her heart, Sandra boarded the plane with Cassandra and Priscilla. She had never flown before and was afraid, but determined not to let the girls know it. Janette, Sharon, Jennie, Arnold, and Dorothy waved to them from the window in the terminal.

After a quick flight to New York's JFK airport and a nonstop flight to Frankfurt, Germany, they were back on the ground again. The first thing out of Frank's mouth was, "If there weren't so many people around, I'd do it right here." Sandra felt nauseous. She suffered excruciating pain in her ears from the descent and they still had to travel another half-hour before reaching the apartment. The last thing on her mind was sex.

That night after they were settled into the apartment, Frank got the sex he wanted. Sandra lay in the bed wanting to reach up into Heaven and go back to the throne room of God. In desperation she prayed for it, her mind stretching as far as it could go. She felt so alone and persistently prayed with a broken spirit and heart.

In response, she was rewarded with a second pass into Heaven's court. The brightness surrounded her as she lay bathed in the warmth of God's love and presence. The experience soon faded away, leaving her comforted, and she fell asleep. Frank never had a clue that anything unusual was happening. He slept in deep unconsciousness.

Later, Sandra realized that this second visit to Heaven was truly a gift from a loving God. She had no right to ask for this blessing because she was still sinning with the fantasies about Elvis. God, in His great mercy and love, forbore His rightful wrath, and instead, gave her the holy desire of her heart.

Army Life

The temporary housing had been a bowling alley at one time. A long hallway split the apartment down the middle with eight rooms available for use as bedrooms. A kitchen, living room, and two bathrooms were cut out of the space at one end. The rooms were simply furnished. Their housing was located on the fourth floor of the officers' quarters.

At Halloween, Frank and Sandra improvised costumes for Cassandra and Priscilla for trick-or-treating. Two bright orange t-shirts bearing the 23rd Battalion logo with a roadrunner, silver ice cream bags with holes cut out for the eyes and mouth as masks, and some plastic bags to collect the candy worked well. As they went door to door, some of the people said, "They're from the 23rd Battalion. Give them more," then dropped extra candy into their bags.

Living in military housing was nice. It was like a small community within a bigger community. When someone had a party, everyone was invited so they could get to know the neighbors. Everyone took turns sweeping and mopping the stairwells and keeping the laundry room clean. The highest ranking officer living in the quarters was in charge of overseeing that the work was done on a rotating basis by the different families.

The local Germans drove around to the housing areas and offered fresh bread, pastries, candy, and beverages for sale almost every morning. Some bruchen (fresh rolls) became a favorite of the Bailey family. Sandra met Carol, one of the officer's wives there and the two became friends.

Carol did macramé. When Sandra expressed an interest in it, Carol offered to show her how. Carol told her what supplies to buy at the commissary and then they made a time for Sandra to come to Carol's apartment for her first lesson. While they visited with each other, their children played. Cassandra was in kindergarten, but Priscilla was still home during the day.

Carol told Sandra about a sale coming up on the following Saturday at the school. It was going to be mostly transformers, which were needed to run the appliances from the United States. (The electricity in Germany and the rest of Europe is 220 volts compared to the 110-115 volts used in the U.S. A transformer stepped down the voltage so electrical products brought over from the U. S. could be used in there. Without one there was no television or other modern conveniences unless the family purchased European appliances.)

Frank and Sandra hadn't purchased a transformer yet because they were so expensive. They were unable to use any of the appliances that had been shipped. Sandra was tempted to go to the sale, but knew she couldn't on Sabbath. She thanked Carol for telling her, and explained why she couldn't go. Carol looked at her strangely, but didn't say anything.

Saturday came and Sandra was tempted to go to the school to check out the transformers. But then she thought, "*God has been too good to me for me to transgress the Sabbath. We'll get a transformer some other way.*" She then dismissed the thought from her mind.

On Tuesday when Frank came home he was all excited about something.

"Guess what I have," he announced.

Sandra didn't have a clue. Frank went back into the

stairwell then returned carrying a huge transformer with six outlets.

"Where in the world did you get that?" Sandra asked incredulously. She knew they didn't have the money to buy one that size.

"I found it in a dumpster," Frank replied. "Somebody moving out just threw it away." It was an older transformer, but it worked. Sandra again recognized God's hand in taking care of their needs and honoring her faithfulness in keeping the Sabbath.

The following spring, Frank was allocated permanent quarters. Every time someone moves out and someone new moves in, the housing and furnishings are checked for damage. Frank and Sandra were instructed to do a walk-thru of their unit with a housing representative. Sandra was glad that an inspection was done because the furniture had been so badly misused it had to be replaced. What once had been an avocado green sofa was now black. The man who lived there was told he would have to pay for it.

The inspector went through the apartment, marking down everything that had to be corrected before they could move in. To allow time to take care of the problems, a final inspection was scheduled at the end of the week.

Sandra watched and kept in mind that they would have to go through the same process when it was time for them to leave. In the meantime, her family was busy cleaning their own quarters. They had already started packing their belongings in anticipation of moving when given the okay to do so.

At the end of the week, they met with the inspector again at the apartment. The previous family had moved out completely. This time, the apartment passed the inspection. Frank signed some papers indicating he would accept the apartment in its clean condition. They moved in that weekend.

Within a few days, a housing representative came by and

showed Sandra some swatches to choose the color of the replacement furniture. This gave Sandra the opportunity to experience how rich people are treated when choosing new upholstery for their furniture. Another dimension was added to her daydreaming.

Preparation for Predicaments

When civilians accompany their military spouses to foreign countries, every effort is made by the military to anticipate possible problems. Civilian spouses had to attend an orientation within a certain period of time. During this orientation, the civilians were given information about local laws, how to get a driver's license, how the local police respond to certain situations with an armed response, and where the offices are located for assistance on the base for housing problems, etc.

Other topics covered marital problems, schools, finances, emotional support, and culture shock. Sandra had never heard of culture shock and listened to the symptoms. Basically, it dealt with being isolated from family and friends with no way to communicate regularly and the inability to communicate effectively in a foreign language with the German community.

"That won't happen to me. I have no reason to feel isolated so much that it would affect me," Sandra thought. She was quite adaptable and felt sure she could handle any situation that might arise. However, the information could be useful if the children should become unsettled, so she listened intently to the instructor.

Hanau, Germany is a beautiful town located one-half hour from Frankfurt. Twice a week a Farmer's Market was held downtown. Sandra would shop there with Cassandra and Priscilla to buy fresh fruits, vegetables, and bread. They rode the city bus to and from the market.

The downtown area had specialty shops for meat, cheese, and baked goods. The small, privately owned shops closed every day for two hours in the afternoon. Department stores were located there as well, which closed around 6 p.m. These limited shopping hours took some getting used to after living in the United States where shopping can go on twenty-four hours a day, seven days a week.

Hanau boasted a local shloss (castle). The family spent weekends going to nearby towns and cities to see different places. They would participate in Volksmarching. A Volksmarch was ten kilometers or 6.2 miles and usually took two to three hours to walk. The route was well-defined by prominent signs with arrows indicating which way to go, which usually wound through a village, into woods, and along the roads. Frank and Sandra enjoyed going on these walks and took the girls with them. A fee was paid and when the Volksmarch was completed the hikers would receive either a meal or collectible plate as an award. There was one walk that stood out from the others.

Frank drove to the town and the Volksmarch started normally. The quaint village was typical. The road led outside the village and wound through the countryside. Everything was going good until they went around the corner of a hill. Suddenly, a gale of wind whipped up. The cool spring air became bitter cold. They struggled against the wind, protecting the girls the best they could. A fine rain drizzled down making them more miserable.

The first checkpoint came into sight and beyond that Sandra saw an old barn. After getting their card stamped, she suggested that she and the girls wait in the old barn while Frank finish the walk and return with the car. He agreed and started running to get there faster. The barn was in a field that bordered a wood where the Volksmarch led. Sandra and the girls huddled together trying to keep warm.

After an hour of waiting, she decided to return to the checkpoint to see if they could get a ride back to the starting point. Frank should have finished the walk by now. They had already gone at least halfway. Sandra became concerned with what might have happened to him.

At the checkpoint they were given hot tea. Sandra could tell one of the women was in charge and approached her with a bit of hesitant German. A car was parked nearby and she wanted to try to get a ride back to the start point.

"Entschuldigen Sie," Sandra said, which meant "Excuse me." The woman looked at her. Sandra struggled to find words to ask for a ride back by trying to describe the situation she was in. „Mein herr get der auto. Ist cold," she said hugging herself to describe the cold, pointing to the children. Shaking her head she said, „Nix herr," then opened her hands and shrugged her shoulders to express that she didn't know where her husband was.

The woman talked with a man there in German then spoke in broken English asking if they needed a ride back. Relief flooded over Sandra as she responded, "Ya bitte," nodding her head yes. The woman motioned for them to come with her and gave them a ride back to the start of the Volksmarch.

After thanking the woman, Sandra took the girls to a large building from which music was playing. She could only wait for Frank to show up. All sorts of bad things kept going through her mind wondering what had happened to him. She had no money and the car was gone, so he evidently had it. They didn't even have any kind of identification on them and she didn't have any phone number to call for help. She was in a foreign country, totally alone with two children, and absolutely helpless.

The German music increased her awareness of her helpless

situation. As she sat on a bench along the wall, she asked the girls if they wanted to sit on her lap. She realized it was more for her own comfort than for theirs. Holding the children, a panic began to rise up in her. She fought it, knowing she couldn't lose control now. It started to overwhelm her and she closed her eyes and hugged the children closer. Just as the feeling was becoming unbearable, she remembered two words: *culture shock.*

Sandra concentrated on what the instructor had said at the meeting. *"This must be culture shock,"* she thought. *"I'm going to be all right."* With the realization of what was happening, it started to subside. The preparation for the emergency was worth more than she could say. If the military hadn't had the meeting, she would not have known what was happening to her. Gratitude to the military for their foresight filled her. A few minutes later, Frank came into the building and found them waiting for him. He explained what had happened.

Upon finishing the Volksmarch, he collected the souvenir medal and got the car to pick them up. However, he drove out of town the wrong way. When he realized that, he tried to turn around and got stuck in some mud. Finally, a couple of other GI's came along and helped him get out of it. When he went back to the spot where Sandra and the girls had been waiting, he found out that someone had given a ride to a woman with two children back to the start.

Sandra remained silent as he told her his story. After he finished, she said, "You know, all you had to do was follow the Volksmarch arrows to where we were waiting."

"That's what I did after I got out of the mud," Frank replied.

Sandra didn't tell Frank about the culture shock experience. She knew he would make light of it and would ridicule her about it. She wasn't going to open herself up to that again if she could help it. Sandra couldn't trust him with her thoughts and feelings. Instead, she found comfort in the fantasy she was currently engaging in and continued it from where she had left off as they drove home.

Sandra learned that day how important it was to be prepared, to know about possible obstacles, not only in physical matters, but also in spiritual matters.

God's Graciousness

When both Priscilla and Cassandra were in school, Sandra had a half day to herself. Priscilla was in kindergarten and came home around 11:30 a.m. Sandra went shopping at the Hanau Kaserne via the shuttle bus provided for military families while Priscilla was in class. One day, realizing it was almost time for the shuttle bus Sandra left the store and went to the bus stop. But the bus didn't come. She started getting concerned because Priscilla was due to be home from kindergarten in about fifteen minutes. She didn't have enough time to walk there as it was more than a mile away and she wasn't in any shape to run the distance as she weighed about 220 pounds.

Finally, she started walking. At the exit of the Kaserne were some signs with the names of the other Kasernes that were within a ten-mile radius. People who had no car would stand by the one they wanted or needed a ride to and wait to see if someone would stop and pick them up. Sandra had never done it before and she hesitated to do it now. She didn't believe it was safe. However, Priscilla was locked out of the house and she needed to get there as fast as she could. Sandra felt impressed to wait by the sign of the Kaserne nearest her housing.

As a car went by, Sandra checked her watch. She was running out of time. Another car went by. She started to leave.

"Wait for the next one," a voice told her.

"Okay, I'll wait for one more," Sandra responded. Another car came. Even if it did pick her up, she still had to walk from the Francois Kaserne to the house which was at least five minutes from there. The driver stopped and offered her a ride. Gratefully, she got in. She and the young man talked along the way. She didn't tell him she had to get home in time to get her daughter, but as they approached the Kaserne, he suddenly asked, "Where do you live? I'll take you home."

Sandra asked, "Are you sure you want to do that?"

He answered, "Sure." Thanking God quietly to herself, Sandra directed the driver to the housing area. They arrived just as Priscilla was getting off the bus. Again, God had provided for her needs, even though she was not living up to all that she knew to be right.

That night, lying in bed, Sandra was convicted that she was not living like she should. She still prayed and believed in God, but was still engaging in her fantasies about Elvis. With great agony in her soul Sandra prayed, "Lord, I know I don't have a right to pray to you. I know I am living with sin in my life. I can't change right now. Please don't give up on me." It gave no comfort, but she felt that God would not forsake her. It was all she could do at the time.

Elvis Speaks

Frank and Sandra often went to the movie theaters and took the children. It was an inexpensive night out that everyone enjoyed. Frank and Sandra were careful about which movies they went to see. They made sure it was "G" rated because they didn't want swearing, sex, or violence in what they watched. Sometimes Sandra would get Frank to watch Cassandra and Priscilla and she would go to a movie by herself.

A movie on the life of Elvis came to the theater at the Francois Kaserne, only five minutes away from their apartment. Sandra wanted to go and asked Frank to watch the girls, which he did. It was 1982, almost five years after Elvis' death.

Near the end of the movie, some footage from one of Elvis' last concerts was shown. He was standing near the piano getting ready to sing "My Way." He shuffled the papers in his hands and then suddenly said, "I'm scared."

Sandra froze in her seat. Her whole body became cold and numb. Instantaneously, the memory of the night at the Paramount Theatre in Glens Falls rushed through her mind. Elvis had received her letters. He had responded by coming to Glens Falls to surprise and meet her. The man in the aisle had asked her "How do you do?" while trying to get her to stop to introduce herself. She remembered the tall man in the shadows bending over to speak to the man that ran to intercept her near the exit. *That man had been Elvis.* The man intercepting her had also asked, "How do you do?" Sandra had not been prepared and lost her chance to meet Elvis. Somehow the letters had invoked a response strong enough for Elvis to make arrangements for the concert to conceal his presence. He had rented the theater and provided the concert just for the purpose of meeting her.

The rest of the movie was a blur. When it was over, she left the theater in numb silence. She was in shock and walked home in a daze. Elvis had answered her letters. There was no doubt about it in her mind. But what good was it to know now? It was too late. Elvis had been dead for almost five years.

At home in bed her mind reeled in confusion and horror. She had written that she had read five etiquette books. They had addressed her correctly, yet she had not responded appropriately.

"How could I have been so stupid?" Sandra writhed in her soul to think what they must have thought of her. They must have had a good laugh at her expense. In utter dejection she lay sleepless deep into the night.

Life didn't give Sandra time to reflect too much on the consequences of her past. Between babysitting and volunteering, taking care of the apartment and bills, she kept on going. Once the initial shock wore off, she again fantasized to escape reality. She added the reality of the Paramount experience into the fantasies. After all, that part was real, but in this way she could change the outcome.

The following year Frank's tour of duty in Germany ended. With new orders to report in Washington, D.C., they left Europe for the United States. As the plane's wheels touched pavement at Fort Dix, New Jersey, a cheer erupted from some of the passengers. Sandra's voice joined theirs. Sandra hadn't planned to cheer; it just involuntarily burst from her.

This was home. A safe place to live. The tension of wondering if Russia or some other country might attack in Europe had always been in the back of Sandra's mind. She had awakened in the middle of one night to what sounded like missile attacks. She woke Frank and told him to listen. He replied, "It's New Year's. Those are fireworks." Here she knew all the customs and when to expect fireworks. Here was where her family was. Here she understood the language and wouldn't need the English-German dictionary to communicate. She felt relief. It was so good to be home.

Starting Again

Frank's orders sent him to the Pentagon as a driver and messenger. Temporary billets were assigned at the Arlington base for two weeks, which gave Frank and Sandra time to find an apartment they could afford. They settled in a complex in Arlington, Virginia, just outside Washington, D.C., and waited for their packages to arrive from Germany.

Sandra had shipped a television and three boxes of personal belongings to Germany. When they left, they had at least a dozen large cartons, as well as furniture, to ship back. Once settled in the apartment, Sandra located a Seventh-day Adventist church to attend. She had missed going to church regularly. In Germany, she had located one near Frankfurt and they had gone sporadically during the three years they were there. The members were transient, due to the nature of the military, and Sandra didn't do well with a lot of change.

Back in the States from Germany, the first time the family went to church was about the time the service was letting out. This was to get the "feel" of the members. It happened that a potluck lunch was being served and they were invited to share it. Sandra listened to the conversations going on around them and found out there was going to be a workbee the next day at the church's Community Services house. She made up her mind to go and help.

Sunday morning Sandra went to the Community Services house and asked what she could do to help. She was directed to a room where ladies were sorting clothing. They all greeted her and introduced themselves. Clothes were in bags all through the house. Sandra found a place to work and started sorting clothes for packing into boxes for shipment.

The Adventist church's worldwide outreach program, ADRA (Adventist Disaster and Relief Agency), sent the clothes to disaster areas. Local churches collected, cleaned, and sorted them by size, season, and gender. The boxes were labeled and every so often a truck came to pick them up. They were taken to the warehouse and kept until needed for distribution.

Sandra held up a see-through nightgown. An elderly woman, Evelyn, remarked, "That's a *see-more* garment." Everybody laughed.

Soon many boxes were packed, labeled, and stacked. Once the supply of boxes ran out, they had to stop working. The house still had rooms full of plastic bags filled with clothes. They would have to wait until more boxes were dropped off when the filled ones were picked up.

The pastor came into the room and asked Sandra who she was. He told her his name was Jim Frost. He was delighted to have a new person helping out with the cleanup. After the work was done, he talked with her about the gifts of the Holy Spirit.

"I know one of your gifts already" he said.

"What's that?" Sandra asked.

"You have the gift of helps," he answered.

Sandra was a little skeptical. Besides, it didn't seem like much of a gift. The pastor went on to say that he'd never met anyone that only had one gift. What he said intrigued Sandra because she had never thought about herself having a gift from God. Even though she had heard it all her life, it hadn't become personal to her. Now someone had recognized a gift from God that she had considered just a part of her character and natural behavior. She enjoyed helping out with projects.

Later, when the church nominated members for offices for the next year, Sandra was asked to be the Community Services Director, and she accepted. She was given a key to the house and the responsibility of having it open for the public. Besides clothing, there was a food pantry for people in need. When Cassandra and Priscilla were in school, Sandra went to the center and worked at washing, sorting and packing clothes. By the time Frank's year was up, there was only one room left with bags of clothes to be sorted.

Sandra walked to and from the center which was about a mile and a half away. The traffic coming out of Washington, D.C. wasn't too bad around 2 p.m. On her way home one afternoon as she was about to step into the street to cross it, she heard someone call her name. She stopped to see who it was and a car that she hadn't seen suddenly turned the corner. If she had stepped into the road, she would have been hit. Looking to see who had called her, there was no one there. Sandra realized it must have been her guardian angel that spoke to her.

Dilemmas

Sandra was still avoiding reality with her fantasies. She told Marsha Frost, the pastor's wife, about some of the disillusionment she felt within her marriage. Marsha made an arrangement for Sandra to meet with a counselor for a one-time session at Marsha's house.

Sandra was unsure about talking to anyone about her problems. She had always handled everything herself and was very introverted. Nevertheless, she hesitantly went to meet with the counselor.

The counselor asked Sandra some questions about her relationship with Frank. Sandra told her about how he sometimes lost control when punishing the girls. She told her about the time she caught Frank peeking at her while she was taking a shower. Sandra had felt like someone was watching her and when she turned around he had his head stuck through the open door watching her. She told him to let her have some privacy.

"So how do you deal with Frank's having sex with you when you don't want him to?" the counselor asked. Sandra was uncomfortable about divulging her secret fantasies.

"I pretend he is someone else," Sandra said cautiously, averting her eyes. The counselor said that was a common practice among women. Sandra was surprised to hear that. It was almost as if she was being given permission to engage in her fantasies. It didn't feel right to her. Sandra knew in her heart it was wrong.

Then the counselor asked her how she felt about God.

"God is the best thing in my life," she answered.

"What do you mean?" the counselor asked.

Sandra talked about what God meant to her. As she did, her face changed. She became excited, glowing with joy.

"I can tell you really love God. Now if you could find a way to maintain your relationship with Frank without feeling like you're compromising your relationship with God, you'd solve your problem," the counselor said.

Not long after her meeting, Sandra confronted Frank and told him she wanted to leave. She was unhappy and didn't want to stay with him. That afternoon they went to the store and a playground with Cassandra and Priscilla. The girls seemed unusually quiet all afternoon. When they arrived home, Frank had to go back down to the car for some things. When he left, Sandra asked them what was wrong. Cassandra didn't say anything, but Priscilla said, "Daddy said if we weren't good you were going to leave us."

Sandra was instantly filled with rage. "Did Daddy tell you that you were bad and I wanted to leave you?" she asked in amazement.

"Yes," Priscilla said.

"Come here," Sandra said. She knelt down and hugged them. "Mommy isn't upset with you. If Mommy goes, you will go with me. You haven't done anything wrong."

After the girls were in bed, Sandra angrily told Frank, "Don't you ever, ever, ever tell these kids that they are the problem between us. How could you tell them they had to be good or I was going to leave them? How could you? This is between us, not them."

Sandra determined to stay with Frank until the girls were old enough to understand that they weren't the problem. She figured out it would take about ten years. Priscilla would be eighteen then and ready to graduate from high school. She had managed to live a double life so far, so she could do it for another ten years for the sake of the children. Unfortunately, she continued to engage in fantasies to avoid her pain, frustration, and anger instead of facing her problems and changing her life.

Full Circle

It has been said that you can't go home. Frank and Sandra returned to Glens Falls. It was the closest they could get. They stayed for a while with Jennie and Arnold. Within a couple of months they had their own apartment in subsidized housing.

Cassandra and Priscilla started school a few days following their move. Sandra worked at McDonald's for a few months and then got a job at a nursing home as an aide. After being put on the graveyard shift, Sandra started looking for another job. She saw a job for sewing machine operators at the unemployment office and went on an interview. She was hired immediately because she had six years' experience and the floor supervisor recognized her from J. & J. Lingerie. She started after a week's notice to her current employer.

When starting a new job, Sandra would tell the employer she could not work on Sabbath hours. She did the same thing now so there wouldn't be a problem later on. Of course, a few weeks later, a meeting was held and the manager informed the employees that mandatory overtime would start that weekend. Sandra approached him with a determined look on her face. He saw her coming.

"That doesn't apply to you," he immediately said.

"Okay," Sandra said and went back to work. Some of the others made comments about it at lunch time.

"It's not just a matter of getting the day off," Sandra said. "It's much more than that. I go to church that day and stay away from stores and doing secular activities on Saturdays." This silenced those who were upset with her "special treatment."

During this time Frank was fired from his job for something he didn't do. When Frank tried to explain what happened to the owner, the man swore at him and told him to leave. After Frank told Sandra what happened, she told him to fight for unemployment because he had been unjustifiably fired. He did and won the case. Within a couple of months he was hired at the James River paper mill in South Glens Falls. This job was one of the best he'd had monetarily. However, it was a swing shift and Frank couldn't keep the Sabbath working it. He chose to keep the job and let spiritual matters go. He also joined the Army Reserves. That took up one weekend a month and two weeks every summer away at camp. The family and marriage became more and more distanced as a result of the separations.

Sandra returned to the church she had attended as a teenager. It was different because a new pastor had come into the area, but there were people there she had known for most of her life. It was like going home.

Working

Sandra worked at C.B. Sports for five years. Charles Byrd Vaughn III had named the business after himself. He had started the business in his garage in Vermont. Wanting to improve ski clothes, he started designing and making his own.

Sandra liked working as a sewing machine operator. She was quick and could run any machine if given a little time to learn it. She was able to earn a decent wage with the piece rates and earned the respect of the management quickly.

The day came when Sandra was given the ultimate task to do. C.B. had gone shopping at the local mall and had purchased a new pair of pants. However, they were too long and needed to be hemmed up. The floor supervisor, Yvonne, gave them to Sandra to hem. It was the highest honor and compliment that could have been given to her as a sewer. A couple of the other sewers watched enviously as she did the work on the pants.

Working at C.B Sports wasn't all work. The employees were a group of women that had fun too. One hot humid Friday, Sandra was eager to go home for the weekend. She was tired and had received her paycheck. With sudden inspiration she cupped her hands by her mouth, making a megaphone, and took a deep breath.

"It's Fridaaaaaaaaaaaaaaaaaaaay!" her voice boomed all the way through the old building, upstairs and down. The other workers turned around to see what was going on. Most of them giggled and made funny comments. From then on, once a week on Friday, she would give her lusty holler.

It became a tradition, even after moving into the new building that C.B. had built. The first week in the new building, someone said to Sandra on Friday, "It's Friday, Sandy."

"Oh yeah," she answered back and then proceeded to deliver her message. A cheer went up among the workers. People from the offices came out to see what was going on. The new building had two floors with the work area closed off from the offices with heavy doors. Yet Sandra's "call" had even reached C.B.'s office at the other end of the building, passing the administrative and human resources offices. Sandra was innocently back to work minding her own business.

In the fall of 1990, rumors started going around that the business was in financial trouble. In November, C.B. called a meeting of all the workers. He introduced some people who had bought into his business and said they would be working with him. However, it was decided to close the factory and send the manufacturing overseas. In January the next year, the plant closed. Everyone went on unemployment.

Building a House—Again

Sandra started work at C.B. Sports in February 1986. That summer Frank and she looked into getting electricity up to the house they had previously built. They were told it would cost $8,000. They decided to look into alternatives so they could have their own home. The Adventist church had a piece of property for sale across from the church for $6,000. The property was approximately 5.2 acres and situated adjacent to the main road. It also bordered their other property. Electricity would cost them almost nothing to hook up, as the local company would come 200 feet from the road without charge.

After checking it out they approached the church board and offered to buy the land. Their offer was accepted and they were able to pay cash for it from the savings bonds they had purchased via monthly automatic deduction while Frank was in the Army.

Frank and Sandra hired an attorney to handle the purchase for them. About a week later, he called and told them an interesting story. The neighbors on the north side of the property were in the process of selling their house. In listing the house, it was discovered that the house had been built partly on the property that Frank and Sandra were purchasing. They actually owned half of the house!

When all was said and done, Frank and Sandra sold a piece of property to the neighbors off from their piece and made $4,000, which gave them a good start for buying materials to build their house. Sandra believed that God had covered this mistake, all those years, just so they would have the money to start with.

During the summer of 1987 it rained by the bucketful. In between deluges, Frank and Sandra worked on getting the cellar built by winter. They hired a contractor to dig the cellar hole and then they built the footing forms and poured concrete. It was so wet and slippery because the ground consisted of heavy clay that one of the cement trucks got stuck. It had to be dragged out by another truck. By the time the cold weather arrived, they still hadn't gotten the cellar cap on, which could ruin the work they had already done.

One day Sandra was talking to Mrs. Foote in church about it and the next day, men started showing up to help cap off the cellar. By the end of the day, the cellar was completely capped off. With the cap on and bad weather coming, work stopped on the house for the winter.

It took two more years before they could move into the house. Even then it wasn't finished completely. The upstairs had no partition walls. The downstairs had plywood floors and bare wallboard on the walls. But they were in their own house and out of the rented apartment. Frank did all the electrical, plumbing, and heating work himself. He would work on the house during the day before working nights on the swing shift.

Now that Sandra was in her own home, she felt able to accept a position at church. When the nominating committee started to meet, she prayed and told God that she would be willing to do whatever God wanted her to do. However, she hoped that she wouldn't be asked to work in the children's division. When she was called and asked to work in the kindergarten room with the 4- to 7-year-old children, she felt a sinking sensation in her stomach, but accepted the position. After all, a commitment to God wasn't something to take lightly.

As time went by, Sandra realized that working in the children's departments was the best thing that could have happened to her. By going back to the basics with songs, stories, and finger plays, her own spiritual foundation had been strengthened and revitalized. But she was still engaging in fantasies to deal with her emotional problems at home.

Christian Companionship

It was at this time in her life that Dency came. Dency had recently moved from Rutland, Vermont to the Glens Falls area. She wanted to be a counselor with the Pathfinders, but didn't have a ride. Sandra volunteered to pick her up on Wednesday nights and give her a ride to the club meetings.

Gradually, they became friends, and after knowing each other for two years, Sandra opened up to Dency and told her about her wonderful experience worshipping at the base of the great white throne in Heaven. Dency accepted her story without faulting her or saying it couldn't be true. It had taken a long time for Sandra to be able to feel she could trust Dency. She had never had a close friendship with other girls growing up or with women, but she was able to start bonding with Dency.

Dency had some unusual spiritual experiences too, which gave them some common ground. Dency said that God had named Jesse, her son, before he was born. She had also had her dead uncle appear to her after his death. When she confronted the evil spirit with the Bible doctrine, "The living know that they shall die, but the dead know not anything" (Ecclesiastes 9:5), the Spirit asked her what she was going to believe. Dency replied that she was going to believe the Bible. The spirit left and never came again.

Dency and Sandra went to the New York Conference Campmeeting together. They borrowed a tent from the Pathfinder Club and pitched it for the week. This was the first Campmeeting Sandra was able to attend. She had wanted to go before this, but every time she brought it up to Frank, he would say they didn't have the money or they had to work. There was always some reason they couldn't go to the week-long retreat held every year.

Pastor George Vandeman was one of the main speakers. Sandra had seen him on television. He was the founder of the "It Is Written" program. She recognized him immediately as he walked by her on the way to his quarters. Impulsively she called, "Pastor Vandeman." He stopped and came toward her. He held out his hand and shook hers. Sandra was conscious of a glow in his face. He looked like Moses must have looked when he came down from the mountain after being with God for forty days and forty nights. She believed that he truly had a loving relationship with God. She began to desire that glow in her life too.

Getting Educated

After Sandra returned from Campmeeting, she became interested in getting some formal vocational training. In her unemployment book, there was a paragraph about training offered to those who lost their job due to having their work sent overseas. Sandra looked into it and found out that a group of employees from C.B. Sports had already filed for the training benefits. She registered for a six-month clerical training class.

Just as she finished the class, her sister Brenda, who worked as an office manager for a local temp office, called her. Brenda offered her temporary employment with a manufacturer of medical catheters as a packager. Sandra was hired as a temp and worked there for five months. After five months, rumors went around that the temps would be laid off due to lack of work.

A few days later, Sandra realized she didn't want to do that kind of work for the rest of her life.

"I know I can do more than package catheters and work in sewing factories," Sandra thought to herself while coiling some catheters for packaging. *"God, if this job ends, I will look into going to college,"* she prayed. Less than two hours later, the

supervisor asked her how she felt about leaving work early that day.

"I don't have a problem with it," Sandra said.

When she left, she went to the unemployment office and asked how to go about getting money for training at Adirondack Community College (ACC). She was told that all she had to do was go to the college and register for classes, which she did.

Sandra went home and announced she was going to college when it started in two weeks. She was already signed up for the Secretarial Science program and would be able to collect unemployment while attending college full time. This was a dream come true for Sandra. She had wanted to go to college for many years. God was providing a college education for her at no cost! And she wouldn't have to work to support herself while getting her education. Two years later, Sandra graduated with a degree in Secretarial Science, Magna Cum Laude.

Growing Girls

Cassandra and Priscilla were growing up before Sandra's eyes. Sandra wished she knew how to communicate better with them. She was so wrapped up with her own emotional and personal problems it was difficult to reach out to them. This soon began to take its toll on them. That summer seventeen-year-old Cassandra dropped a bombshell.

Cassandra and Sandra were walking in a department store when Cassandra said, "I think I'm pregnant." Sandra paused and glanced at Cassandra, who was looking in the other direction. It amazed Sandra how much Cassandra was like her and needed to avoid conflict.

"What makes you think that?" Sandra asked casually while looking at some clothes on the rack. This was not a moment she had been looking forward to. She had to handle it carefully. The last thing she wanted to do was to alienate Cassandra with some stupid remark or hurt her.

"I haven't had my period for three months," Cassandra responded.

"Then I guess we need to make an appointment with a doctor and get you checked out."

Sandra knew Cassandra was sexually active because late one evening in January, she had heard unusual noises in

Cassandra's room which was above the master bedroom. Finally she got out of bed and went upstairs. Sandra knocked on Cassandra's door and tried to turn the knob. The door was locked, which it had never been before.

Sandra heard some voices and movement and then Cassandra opened the door. Sandra smelled some smoke.

"What is that smoke I smell?" Sandra asked. Cassandra answered quickly, too quickly, "That's from the fire when I burned the garbage." Sandra wasn't comfortable with the answer or the movements she had heard a few moments prior.

"Is someone in here with you?" Sandra asked as she entered the room. Sandra went to the closet and opened it. A young male stood there with only a pair of pants on.

"Frank, there's someone in Cassandra's room!" she yelled. The boy ran past Sandra, down the stairs, and out the door before Frank could get to him. She had never seen anyone run so fast in her life.

The boy went out into the bitter cold night without shoes or shirt. It was snowing and freezing rain. Sandra called the sheriff and about half an hour later they drove up to the house asking for the boy's clothes. He was sitting in the back seat of the patrol car. The sheriff had been getting calls from several of the neighbors because he had been knocking on doors trying to get someone to let him in.

Frank and Sandra sat down with Cassandra and talked with her about the baby. They asked if she was planning on keeping it or putting it up for adoption. Cassandra wanted to keep the baby. Sandra told her she would support her decision. Even though Frank said he would support Cassandra's decision, he became angry about the pregnancy. He felt betrayed and hurt by his daughter. His actions and words were hurtful to everyone in the house.

Cassandra started her senior year at school that fall in the Hudson Falls public school. Priscilla chose to go to Union Springs Academy (USA), the high school run by the Seventh-day Adventists in Union Springs, New York.

Although the school was over two hundred miles from home, Sandra was glad Priscilla wanted to go there. She wrote to Priscilla and sent "care" packages through the mail.

Sandra's emotional status became more and more unstable. The fantasies were becoming so ingrained in her mind that sometimes she didn't know where she was. She'd wake at night and lay in bed trying to get a grip on her surroundings. After a few minutes she'd realize she was still in bed with Frank in the house they had built in Hudson Falls.

Scared, she prayed to be able to get away from fantasizing. It would work for a little while, then unwilling to deal with the realities of her unhappy life, she hid her pain and hurt in fantasizing again. With Frank becoming more miserable with Cassandra's pregnancy, Sandra began to feel desperate to get out again. However, she struggled with the idea of leaving after putting so much into building the house and investing so many years in the marriage.

Frank was unaware and unconcerned about her emotional well-being. They had watched the Gary Smalley tapes, "Keys to Loving Relationships" together. Sandra had tried to use the concepts presented in the tapes for communication, but she was unable to get Frank to understand what she was trying to say. The deep issues she had were never addressed.

The weekend before Thanksgiving, Frank had Army Reserve meetings. On Sunday morning, he "took" sex and then left. Sandra lay in the bed emotionally, mentally, and spiritually drained. She was tempted to get the .22-caliber rifle in the closet and blow her brains out. It would be easy enough. She knew how to load it and put it into her mouth. But then she knew she couldn't go to Heaven when Jesus returned if she did that. For the commandment states, "Thou shalt not kill."

"Okay, Lord. Here I am. What do I do now?" Sandra asked desperately.

"Call Gary Bombard," the answer came back.

The day before in church, Gary said he had an apartment for rent. Sandra called and asked if she could rent it. After receiving Gary's approval, Sandra went upstairs to Cassandra's room and knocked on the door.

"I'm leaving your father. Do you want to come with me?" she asked.

"Yes," Cassandra said immediately getting up.

"Then pack your clothes. We need to move our stuff while he's at Reserve duty," Sandra said. She went downstairs and started packing her things.

"At least Priscilla won't have to deal with any of this. She is safe in Union Springs," Sandra thought to herself. By the time Frank came home, they were gone.

Sandra and Cassandra lived in Gary's apartment for a couple of months. Because Sandra only had unemployment for income, she was eligible for subsidized housing and they moved as soon as they could.

Brenda came to visit Sandra and gave her money to help out. Janet sent money from Georgia too. Sandra was surprised and very thankful for her sisters' support.

Frank kept trying to get Sandra to come back to him. Finally, she agreed to Christian counseling. Frank located one and made an appointment for them to go. Before the first visit, Sandra told Frank she wanted the second half hour with the counselor by herself.

When Pastor Maitha asked what the problem was, Frank answered, "She has a problem." After Frank left the room, the pastor asked, "Did you hear what he said?"

"Yes," Sandra said, "He said, 'She has a problem.' He doesn't believe that he has any problems. It's all me."

It turned out that Frank and Sandra were co-dependent. Pastor Maitha explained that this kind of relationship doesn't usually last as long as this one did.

"How have you lasted so long?" he asked.

"I have God in my life," Sandra answered.

Unfortunately, Sandra never did reach a level of comfort

with Pastor Maitha to tell him about the fantasies. Most of the sessions, she listened to Frank talk and tell his life's story. Then he would refuse to acknowledge he needed to address the problems in his life.

Pastor Maitha asked Sandra what she thought of college, since she was almost forty years old and just now attending.

"It's like my mind has been in a little black box all these years and now it's opened and I'm never going to go back into it again," Sandra replied making the shape of a box with her hands. Pastor Maitha said he liked that analogy.

After several months of counseling, Sandra agreed to move back into the house, but only if Jennie moved out. Frank agreed and told his mother she had to move out, which caused some hard feelings for a while.

Sandra was starting to learn how to make her life better. Unfortunately, some decisions had to be made that would make others unhappy. It was all part of learning and growing.

During the next summer, Sandra realized that the counseling wasn't helping her. Frank tried to get her to go to Pastor Maitha's office, but she refused. Sandra suggested that Frank go since the time had already been paid for. He went that one time and didn't go again. But why should he, after all he didn't have any problems.

Reality Pulverization

For the next four years, to compensate for her personal mental and emotional deficiency, Sandra became more and more involved with the church as her life deteriorated. She was elected as the Community Services Director, which gave her opportunities to assist less fortunate people. She volunteered as a counselor with the Pathfinders (an organization similar to the Scouts). Sandra also taught the Junior Sabbath School class every week, and helped out with other functions as asked or needed. She was doing all of this on top of working full time.

That summer Sandra decided to lose weight. She tipped the scale at over 250 pounds. She knew what to do and started by walking every morning at the gym of the Adventist school. As a board member she had the keys to the building. By November she lost 10 pounds.

On November 6, 1997, Unsolved Mysteries aired a special on Elvis's death. During the program, Sandra saw Rick Stanley reveal giving Elvis drugs on the morning of August 16, 1977. He said that Elvis asked him to pray with him. The actor portraying Elvis kneeled on the floor.

Sandra watched, horrified, as Rick Stanley, Elvis's stepbrother, re-enacted the events from the evening before

Elvis's death. The portrayal stated that Elvis saved an injection and then waited until the time for the next one, taking both at the same time. With the double dose of drugs, it was too much for his system to handle and he died from the overdose.

In stunned silence Sandra watched the actor kneel to pray. In instantaneous replay, her mind returned to the years before when Elvis had been in the Paramount Theatre and Rick Stanley had addressed her there just as she was exiting the building. Her trip part way to Las Vegas with strangers giving her money to help and encourage her. Her fear causing her to turn around. Elvis' last desperate plea from the stage at his last concert that she heard during the movie in Germany. Then six weeks later his death.

All these thoughts and more furiously attacked her conscience with an unrelenting savagery. And suddenly she knew that Elvis had taken the dosage in the desperate hope that he would be readmitted to the hospital, that the news would reach her ears causing her to write to him again. There was no doubt in her mind of this conclusion.

In awful; convulsive; grief-stricken remorse, she sobbed uncontrollably. She had reached out the hand of friendship to Elvis. For three and a half years, he had been thinking about her letters and their failed introduction. He had tried to contact her through his concert with his humiliating confession, "I'm scared." Now in a last desperate attempt to get her attention, he had overdosed unintentionally. He had miscalculated the amount of drugs his body could handle and it killed him. And she realized she was partially to blame for his death. Elvis **was** searching for spirituality!

Overwhelming consternation filled Sandra with the truth that Elvis had tried to contact her. He'd read her letters, responded to them by going to Glens Falls, and three and a half years later, he tried to get her to contact him again.

Inexpressible grief welled up inside Sandra. She'd failed God in His attempt to reach Elvis. Her whole life of faith had been for naught. Elvis's needs had been unmet and God had wanted her to help him. Uncontrollable pain filled Sandra. She became completely unhinged with her failure to this man whom she had spent over twenty years fantasizing about. Unable to comprehend the depths of Elvis's humiliation to reach out, *on the stage, before twenty thousand fans*, to try to get her, *her,* to respond to his cry for help, Sandra collapsed on the bed fully clothed and agonized until she could weep no more.

Words cannot describe the utter agonizing remorse and regret that Sandra experienced that night. Her friendship had been accepted. The letters had reached a part of Elvis that he wanted and needed to have responded to, and she failed him. With supreme sobs, unlike any she had ever experienced before, she lay crumpled up on her bed and cried.

In the morning Sandra stumbled out of bed, put on her sweatshirt and sweatpants, and went to the gym to walk. It was different this time. Guilt-ridden with the memories flooding through her mind, she walked and cried as the music played. She'd failed a person to whom she had offered friendship. The weeping reached an uncontrollable point so that she had to stop and lean on the wall as the sobs overcame her body. She felt as if her heart was going to burst with the pain.

Exhausted after the workout, Sandra went home and showered. Again sobs came. It was a good thing that she had no children to watch and no job to go to for there was no way she could have handled them at this time.

It wasn't just the fact that Elvis had come to meet her or that she had failed to help him when he needed her. She was also overcome with the love of God for his forgiveness in her failing Him as well, for she had failed God. All too clearly she now understood—the strangers truly indeed had been angels sent to encourage her to continue the journey to Las Vegas to meet Elvis. The angel had pushed down on her head and shoulder and whispered in her ear, "Kneel, kneel" in the Paramount Theatre. God had truly been trying to get her to meet Elvis. And for the three and a half years following her letters, she could have walked up to the gate of Graceland to introduce herself and she would have been invited in without any hesitation from Elvis.

Oh, the utter devastation to her soul at this revelation! *"If only, if only, if only I had known! Oh God, why didn't I see it? Why was I soooo stupid? How could I have been so dumb?"* she thought, tormented by her failure to both God and Elvis.

Between November 6, 1997, and January 1, 1998, Sandra lost twenty pounds just from grief. She had to force herself to eat. She realized that God in His mercy had allowed her to live. He had already forgiven her. He had accepted her praise and prayers and allowed her to worship Him at the base of His great white throne. She had been forgiven even before she knew about her sin.

When Sandra realized God's mercy, her grief intensified. "How could You possibly forgive me for such a terrible sin?" she asked while walking at the gym one morning.

"Because I love you," Jesus spoke gently to her. She believed that if Elvis and she had met, he would have listened to the Bible truths that she knew. She had no doubt about it. He was searching for truth and she could have helped him find it. With his conversion, possibly millions would also have been influenced to study their Bibles and come to the conclusion about the truths there. And in all possibility, with millions converted, the final conflict between good and evil could have been finished, and Jesus would have already come. Sandra carried the weight of the world on her shoulders.

Recovering enough to walk, Sandra went home and took a shower. Again, the remorse and regret coursed through her. The tears of grief mingled with the water of the shower. Exhausted, she had to go back to bed and get some sleep.

As the days went by, each one became like the first. Sandra's life had become irrevocably changed. The walking now became an exercise in outrunning the Devil as he tormented her for failing to finish the trip to Las Vegas and instilling her with the fear that had kept her from going to Memphis in 1974.

But as much as the Devil tormented Sandra, Jesus comforted her. Sandra struggled with her inability to do anything about what had happened. She asked God how He could still want her after her enormous lack of faith. But texts from the Bible coursed through her mind as she questioned God.

"How can you still want me to be in Heaven with you God?" Sandra agonized.

"Because I love you," He answered (Luke 16:27).

"But I failed you—and Elvis—as he searched for help."

"In times of ignorance God winks," God responded (Acts 17:30).

As God gave her the assurance that He knew that she hadn't known all that was happening at the time, Sandra's heart became even more broken. She determined that the fantasizing would stop. She didn't want to keep on hurting God, especially since He had forgiven her for the many years of failure and mistakes.

Sandra recognized that God had forgiven her. She was able to look back and remember the experience of worshipping God at the base of His great white throne in Heaven when she lived in Texas. So many times she had wondered why He had allowed that to happen to her. If He hadn't already forgiven her, even before she knew about her great failure, He would have never allowed her to approach His holy throne in Heaven for any reason.

Knowing these things did not bring comfort to Sandra. She suffered greatly for not obeying God. Gradually, as she was able to bear the immensity of what she had not done, God revealed to her that if she had gone to Memphis, Elvis would have listened and converted. Not only he, but millions of other people would have been influenced by the changes in his life.

Unbearable sorrow came with this knowledge. In agony of

soul Sandra cried out, "I cannot bear this!" God immediately responded to her cry, "My grace is sufficient for thee" (II Corinthians 12:9).

The weight of the whole world rested upon Sandra's shoulders. If it weren't for her disobedience, God would have come to take His people back to Heaven by now and Elvis would still be alive. Millions would NOT make it to Heaven because of her fear and stupidity.

Out of grief, loss, and her sudden understanding of the immeasurable love of God, Sandra lost 20 pounds in two months. She had to fight herself and make herself eat. She had to live. Dying now would only bring more dishonor to God. All the beings in Heaven knew of her failure and God's attempt to send her to Elvis to help him. Elijah, Moses, and all the resurrected saints from Jesus' resurrection knew of her failure. All the beings on the other worlds created by God knew of her failure. She had to live to "redeem the time"(Colossians 4: 5) left to her.

In November Sandra started working as a home health aide in the private homes of elderly people. She still had to work to support herself in spite of the racking emotional pain she was going through. That job gave her an income and the privacy she needed to weep whenever she had to.

Sandra read again *The Great Controversy* by Ellen G. White. She realized more fully the times she was living in. Living in the home of an elderly woman on the weekends, she was thankful that God had given her a job where she could be alone most of the time. She knew He was sheltering her, just as He had when her father died by letting her stay with Mabel and Arthur during her time of grief. And when Elvis had died, she had suddenly come down with bronchitis and missed a whole week of work because she was sick. God had made a way for her to grieve at those times.

Sandra prayed and asked for complete victory over the fantasies that had controlled her life for over twenty years. Satan attacked her over and over again, trying to get her to indulge in her weakness. Satan reminded her that it was too late to help Elvis now, so why not continue to fantasize about him? With Satan's temptations came the full realization that if it hadn't been for Satan making her fearful in the first place, she would have met Elvis. He no longer had any power over her.

Sandra realized all that Jesus had sacrificed for her. For not only had He died for her, but He also had forgiven the mistakes she made which cost Him many souls for His kingdom. Sandra's heart was touched when she read, "Since thou wast precious in my sight, thou hast been honorable, and I have loved thee; therefore will I give men for thee, and people for thy life" (Isaiah 43:4). Sandra began to love Jesus for the forgiveness and mercy He had bestowed upon her.

Sandra hated herself for the fear and lack of faith she had had. God, Jesus, and the Holy Spirit never criticized her for the past failures she was responsible for. She only received messages of hope, comfort, and love. As she struggled with the remorse and pain, she turned to the Bible for comfort. As the great love of the Holy Ones of Heaven became more revealed to her, her heart became even more broken. In utter anguish and complete surrender, she could only take hold of their love and grasp the Hand held out to her in great pity and mercy.

When Sandra realized that Jesus knew before He left Heaven all that she would do even before He died for her, she asked Him why He was still willing to let her live. He responded, "Because I love you and want you to live in heaven with Me forever." In great humiliation and contrition, her heart broke. She had nothing and no one to cling to except God. Over and over again God reassured her of His love and forgiveness.

Sandra's life had been ruined. Her marriage was a mess, in large part because she refused to deal with conflict. She had run away from her pain and purpose. Unable to undo what had been done, she threw herself upon the unfathomable mercy of God and He loved and accepted her.

Just before Christmas, Sandra tried to reconcile with
Frank. They started living together again. She believed that
it was more her fault that the marriage hadn't worked out,
so she gave it one more chance. They'd had counseling and
she really tried to see things his way. She met him more than
halfway to work out the reconciliation.

Priscilla came back for Christmas from her job as a nanny
near New York City and invited a friend to stay for a couple of
days. When Sandra started tearing up while cooking in the
kitchen, Priscilla told her friend, "My mom is so sentimental
at Christmastime." Sandra didn't say anything to her and
kept on working. If that was how Priscilla perceived her
grief, she wasn't going to contradict her. Sandra hadn't yet
told Priscilla or anyone else what was going on. She felt that
just because she was suffering intensely that was no reason to
drag everybody else down into her private hell.

In the meantime, Sandra had started working at Sears
for the Christmas holiday season as a second job. She was
assigned to the Domestics Department. Every time she saw
king-size sheets, pillows, pillowcases, comforters, and other
items, a pang went through her heart. It wasn't the sheets
per se that were so traumatizing as the fact that Elvis had
been heralded as the king of rock n' roll. The association
was tormenting.

At work, Christmas music played over the intercom, some
of it Elvis'. Sandra struggled so hard to keep from bursting
into tears, but she couldn't stop them. Agony of mind and
heart constantly tormented her. A person she cared about
wanted her to help him, yet she was not aware of his need.

Every day she struggled with the past. Every day while
walking, working, and driving, the memory churned through
her mind. Time after time, the scenes from the Paramount
Theatre played. Then in graphic detail, the last days of Elvis'
life haunted her every waking moment. He'd humiliated
himself before his audience to try to get a message to her and
then waited in hopeful anticipation to get a letter. Six weeks

later, in desperation, he took the additional dosage of drugs. He was alone, scared, desperate, hopeless, and unhappy. And she was the only one in the whole world that he felt could help him. "Oh God," she cried. "I can't go on like this."

Jesus answered, "My grace is sufficient for thee" (II Corinthians 12:9) and "All things work together for good to them that love God and are the called according to His purpose" (Romans 8:28).

Sandra questioned, "How can this be for the good?"

And again her response came, "All things work together for good to them that love God and are the called according to His purpose." She had to accept the answer, even though she didn't understand it.

In December Sandra applied and was hired for a job as a receptionist with Washington County. With the extreme psychological torment she was undergoing, the job was the best thing that could have happened. It gave her something new to learn and concentrate on, keeping her mind occupied during the time she was there. Even though the job helped, she was still often reminded of Elvis. Her supervisor's name was Lisa (Elvis's daughter's name). The number for the safe contained 42 as part of the combination (Elvis's age at his death).

Sandra wanted to call in to a counseling program on the radio, but didn't for fear that a group of psychiatrists would come and put her in a straight jacket and lock her up for claiming to be partially responsible for the death of Elvis Presley. She hadn't lost her mind yet. Instead, she wrote to Red West, Elvis's cousin, in care of Elvis Presley Enterprises in Memphis, Tennessee:

***

Dear Mr. West:

There are many strange things that happen during our lifetimes. One such incident has occurred to me. I would like to relate my story to you and request that you try to help me piece the puzzle together.

In the spring of 1974, I wrote some letters to Elvis. Little did I know how he would answer my letters. I spoke of everyday things, such as the weather, his work as an entertainer, God, and the Bible. I even asked him if he ever got stage fright. I did not at first give my return address on the letters, but later decided to do so.

Soon after writing to Elvis with my return address, a religious concert was held at a local theater in Glens Falls, New York, where I lived at the time. After the concert was over, I was approached by two different gentlemen who addressed and asked me, "How do you do?"

Thinking they we just being polite, I answered, "Fine thank you, how are you?" to each of them. I had no idea of who they were and was not looking for anyone to approach me for any reason at that time. I was very young and naïve, not realizing until much later that Elvis was there and had gone there specifically to meet me.

This would have been the end of it, except at Elvis's last concert he made a reference to the stage fright question in my letter stating, "I'm scared" while on stage. Unfortunately, I was not at the concert when he tried to contact me. I did not know of his attempt until after his death. Of course, it was too late for me to respond then.

I have tried to push these things to the back of my mind all these years. However, there was an episode of "Unsolved Mysteries" which aired on, November 6, 1977, showing a reenactment of Elvis's death, which made me unable to do so anymore. It seemed as though the gentleman relating the re-enactment was angry. I think his name was Gary. I understand his anger.

I am unable to remove the memory of Elvis asking for my help from the stage. If I had known he was so desperate for help, I would have contacted him immediately. I believe that I could have helped him. I have been suffering from guilt for not being there for him when he needed someone to help him.

I would like to ask the gentlemen who were with Elvis that night in Glens Falls if they would be willing to meet with me so that I may discuss what happened at that time. I do not know who they are and have no way of contacting them myself. There is also more information that I would like to share with them. I also have many questions that only they can answer for me because they were the only other ones who were there at that time and knew what was going on.

I have provided my address, work phone number, and home phone number for your convenience. I would be very grateful for your help in arranging these meetings. If necessary, I am willing to travel to a more convenient place for the meeting. I do not expect everyone to come to me.

Thank you for your time and consideration.

Respectfully yours,

Sandie

***

Sandra never received a response to her letter. After so many years, what good would it have done anyway?

Sandra knew she needed help, but didn't know how to get it and had no money to pay for any. Besides, there was no way to tell someone else in a short hour the depths of the agony she was experiencing. How does one explain their failure to God and to another person? What does one say to express conviction of soul in a way that makes sense?

And so she turned to God. She threw herself into more church work. She had to do anything she could to "redeem the time" she had wasted. All those years, she could have been doing something positive instead of just existing and living day by day. Sandra became the Stewardship Secretary and Community Services Director at church and volunteered to organize a Vacation Bible School. When a Revelation Seminar aired via satellite, she volunteered to run a program for the children so the parents could see the seminar without interruption.

Every morning at the gym the grief and unbearable remorse took control of her as she power-walked. As the conviction and guilt pressed upon her mind, she would force herself to go as fast as she could. It was as if the very demons of Hell were chasing her around the gym. This went on for almost two years.

During that time, Sandra did finally talk to her daughter Priscilla about her failure to meet with Elvis. One day they were sitting at the table in the kitchen and tears started to glisten in Sandra's eyes. Priscilla said, "Let it go. It happened a long time ago. There's nothing you can do about it now."

Sandra said, "They knew who I was. Two different men tried to contact me. You don't understand, Priscilla. If I had met Elvis and he changed his lifestyle through my influence, he would have influenced millions. Because I didn't, those people may not be in Heaven."

Priscilla understood better what was bothering her mother, but still insisted that she needed to "get over it." Since Priscilla felt she should just drop the matter, Sandra kept silent about it after that.

Eventually, Sandra gave Frank a brief description of Elvis's trip to Glens Falls to meet her. He voiced that she had no proof and in essence he really didn't believe her. However, Frank claimed he went to the town hall to find out if there were any records available about the Paramount Theatre. He said that since the building had been destroyed, no records were available for concerts held there so long ago. Sandra felt he had inquired about the records only to satisfy his own curiosity. She found no comfort in his attempt to "help" her.

In her attempts to tell her family about the incident, Sandra did not explain about the angel who pressed her head and shoulders and spoke to her. The whole experience was pretty unbelievable after all. If she couldn't explain what happened to them, who else would be willing to listen? She never received a response from Red West.

Without anyone to talk to, Sandra remained silent and

tried to make sense of everything that had happened. The Bible became her comforter. "All things work together for good to them that love God and are the called according to his purpose" (Romans 8:28), became her constant comfort. And when the pain became unbearable and she cried out to God saying, "I cannot bear this anymore," Jesus replied again as He told the apostle Paul, "My grace is sufficient for thee" (II Corinthians 12:9).

And because Sandra realized how much she had been responsible for, she accepted her plight. She had been blessed with much, forgiven much, and loved very much by the God she had hurt and grieved by her unbelief.

Rationalization

In trying to make sense of what had happened, Sandra began to analyze the sequence of events surrounding Elvis's trip to Glens Falls. The men who were with Elvis knew what was going on, even if she didn't. The second man that intercepted her was the one on the "Unsolved Mysteries" program. He was also the one who had come to help Bob in the park when he'd had his seizure.

The strange look on his face kept coming back to haunt Sandra. *"What had he been thinking?"* she wondered. *"What did he see in my face to give him such a reaction to me? Was it the glowing happiness I was experiencing? Was he surprised to see someone so young? Was that it? Did he think I was just a teenager? After all, he had no way of knowing that I would have my twenty-first birthday that June."*

If that was the case, then the whispering outside her door made sense too. In her contemplations, Sandra suddenly realized that he would have told the others that she was too young and would be "jail bait" for Elvis. In this way, he could protect both Elvis and her. It was the only explanation she could deduce.

Sandra felt that a man of Elvis's caliber must have had some kind of emotional investment in her to keep her in his mind for the next three and a half years. That's a long time for someone to remember another person only through the contact of a few letters. This too increased her pain. She felt she had betrayed another human being, one that Jesus had died for. One that she believed she cared deeply about too.

The words from one of Elvis's songs came back to haunt her: "The fire of love, the fire of love, can burn from afar; and nothing can light the dark of the night like a falling star." (*Summer Kisses, Winter Tears* from the *Let's Be Friends* album) Had Elvis romanticized about her as she had about him? What could have kept her in his mind for so long without any other contact? These questions plagued her waking moments.

As the scenes from the "Unsolved Mysteries" played in her mind, all she could think was, *"Elvis tried to contact me because of the spiritual content of my letters. He had prayed shortly before dying that day. He had asked the man with him to kneel and pray with him."*

By the time night arrived, Sandra would close her eyes and immediately fall asleep from the weariness that came from the memories that flooded her mind all day. She was utterly exhausted by the time she went to bed. Mercifully, sleep gave her the only release from the tormenting thought that if she hadn't been so afraid, Elvis would still be alive.

The Final Insult

That April Sandra endured a highly stressful period. She was still trying to keep her marriage from falling apart, working, volunteering at the church, and running a household. Frank wasn't working, so the full responsibility for the bills fell upon her shoulders. Sometimes he did work part time, but not enough to count on the money regularly.

Frank was preparing for rebaptism on Easter weekend. Sandra was still trying to deal with her own emotional pain and one evening Frank wanted to have sex with her. She told him she wasn't up to having sex as she was concerned about Cassandra that evening. Sandra had been avoiding going to bed with him anyway, as their reconciliation had become very difficult for her. After she went to bed that evening, he kept pestering her for sex. Sandra told him she wasn't interested. Then he said angrily, "I wish they would legalize prostitution."

Sandra lay stunned, unable to process exactly what his words implied. Then he forced her to have sex as she lay there unresponsive. In shocked horror all Sandra could do was pray, "Father forgive him because he doesn't know what he is doing" and finally fell asleep.

The next morning Sandra went to the gym. While walking,

she reflected on what had happened the night before. The more she thought about it, the angrier she became. By the time she walked home, she had sorted out the implications of his "prostitution" comment. When Sandra returned home, Frank was outside just leaving for work. As he approached her, Sandra, in barely controlled fury, told him, "You are not touching me again, ever!" Her left arm hung straight and stiff. Her right hand, tightly clenched with a finger pointing at him, thrust into his face. She repeated to him what he had said to her and concluded with, "I am nothing but a prostitute to you! After thirty years of marriage, that's all I am!" Frank told her he had not said that. Then he said she had heard something he had not said and that she had turned his words around. He followed her into the house and told her she had no right to upset him as he was leaving for work.

At that Sandra turned around and with her fist in his face told him in a clear, cold, calculated voice, "Get away from me or I will go into the closet, get the rifle, and blow your f@#! head off!!!" Her voice rose in a furious tirade and if looks could kill, Frank would have been dead. Frank looked at her. Sandra was livid. He had never seen her like this before. Without replying, Frank had already turned around and left the house. When Sandra returned from work that evening, Frank moved his personal clothing, belongings, and the rifle upstairs to Cassandra's old bedroom. And Sandra was true to her word. She never allowed him to touch her sexually again. They lived in the same house for over two years in separate bedrooms.

That weekend Frank was rebaptized. Both of their families were invited to come. At the time of his baptism they were asked to stand in recognition of his recommitment. Sandra stood and felt like a hypocrite. However, she kept her mouth shut about their relationship with each other.

During the following months, members of the church started talking to Sandra about Frank again. He had been talking to them and trying to get their sympathy aroused.

Sandra knew what was going on and refused to talk to anyone about the trouble between them. Besides, he was doing enough talking for both.

Pastor Manning had died after suffering from a brain tumor. A new just recently ordained pastor was hired to take his place. Pastor Hrovat and Sandra spoke a little one evening at his request because Frank had asked him to talk to her. She went to the church office and they spoke about marriage. The only thing she told him was that Frank had crossed a line that could not be withdrawn. Several months later, they were discussing the bulletin (Sandra was bulletin secretary) and he brought up Frank again. This time she said, "You want to know what he said to me? I'll tell you." After she told him, he didn't even blink.

Pastor Hrovat then admitted to Sandra that Frank had already told him that within the first week he arrived. It only confirmed her anger against Frank. He was spilling out very private matters to a stranger, although a pastor, at the first chance he could get.

Sandra asked Pastor Hrovat if he would tell his fiancée that and how his fiancée would feel if he had said those words to her. He saw her point.

When Frank and Sandra spoke later, she said to him, "Do you think that talking about me to everybody is going to make things better? You are making things worse. So if you want to talk, go ahead." And she walked away.

The following year, Sandra went to the doctor for a pap smear and physical. She was told she was losing blood and was sent to have an ultrasound done. When it came back, her doctor told her she needed to see a gynecologist. At the gynecologist's she was told she needed to have a hysterectomy as she had a fibroid tumor about four inches in size.

The surgery was scheduled for February 2, 1999. Sandra had no fear of the surgery. After it was over, Priscilla and Cassandra were in her room waiting for her. Priscilla took one look at her and started crying, and left the room for a couple of minutes. Cassandra looked shocked to see her mother in such a state, but controlled her emotions. In spite of her half-conscious condition, Sandra realized again that Cassandra was a lot like her in that way

Cassandra and Priscilla didn't stay long as Sandra was very tired. Pastor Hrovat came by to read a Scripture and pray for her. Sandra was glad to see him. He came by every day that she was there. Other visitors were her mother and friends Dency, Dona, Holly, and Rosemary. Frank came but she made him leave. He had showed up before the surgery on the day of the operation, but she made him go then too.

Before going into the hospital, Sandra had bought a little diary to write about her experience. She was actually looking forward to getting it done. As a Seventh-day Adventist, she understood that there would be "a time of trouble such as never was" (Daniel 12:1) before Jesus comes again. She had wondered how she would get through that time and have to deal with her menstruation problem. The hysterectomy solved that concern for her.

Through the benefits package at the county, Sandra was able to spend four weeks at home to recuperate with pay by using all her saved up vacation, sick, and personal time.

While at home Sandra had time to continue to grieve. As she was grieving one day, she heard Jesus say, "As the humiliation and shame of the cross have become my glory, so your shame will become your glory." Sandra wept with the precious promise that Jesus had given her. He was still with her and wanting to comfort her sorrow, regret, and remorse.

Later, Sandra received confirmation of this through reading an article written by a former homosexual. He married a woman, having overcome his sexual tendencies after converting to Christianity, testifying to God' power. In his article, he said that his shame had become his glory.

In the Bible, it was in the laws of the Israelites that there must be at least two witnesses at a trial. The word of one witness was not enough in matters involving the death penalty (Deuteronomy 17:6). Sandra had two witnesses to proclaim that her shame would one day become her glory. The immeasurable love of God continued to give her hope. Sandra came to know the height, depth, breadth, and length of God's love for her and for everyone living on this earth. For if God loved *her* like that, then He loves every other human being just as much.

Reaching Out & Jesus Speaks

A whole month off from work! While browsing through the Internet, Sandra decided to look up Wayne Newton's Web site. She had seen an advertisement that he was coming to the Glens Falls Civic Center. After looking up his schedule, she felt impressed to write to him. In the letter, she invited him and his entourage to come to church on the morning of his concert, as he would be performing on a Saturday evening. Enclosed with the letter were directions, and a map to the church. She assured him that she would not contact the press or tell anyone so he could come without being harassed. Sandra received no communication from him; however, the day she had invited them to come, two people, a man and a woman came for Sabbath School that she didn't recognize. They were tall, thin, and deeply tanned, or possibly of Native American descent. When she introduced herself, they didn't identify themselves as being associated with Mr. Newton, so she didn't ask. She felt she would probably never know if they were. She was still recuperating from the surgery and looked drawn at the time.

All during this time, Sandra continued to lose weight. After Frank's baptism on Easter weekend, one of the women who worked with her brought in some chocolate-covered caramels.

Sandra took two. On her way to pick up the mail, she bit into the second caramel and then clearly heard the Holy Spirit say gently, "Chocolate offends Me." Sandra finished the caramel and then replied, "If that's the way it is, then that's the way it is." She made up her mind not to eat chocolate any more. She didn't want to offend the Holy Spirit.

About a month later of going without chocolate, Sandra was driving down the road. It suddenly hit her that she would have a problem at Halloween. The sudden thought brought panic as she remembered a certain confection that only came out during the Halloween season. She called them "orange pumpkins." She was alone in her van and said out loud, "Lord, chocolate is one thing, but orange pumpkins are something else." She panicked knowing how much she liked to eat these candies.

Immediately, Jesus spoke to her, "Sandra, I have something so much better for you in Heaven than orange pumpkins." The panic went away. Sandra sobbed gratefully to Jesus for His direct intercession on this problem. The promise of being in Heaven with Him and the knowledge that He would overcome the chocolate for her was so intensely sweet. She never did have any inclination nor desire to eat orange pumpkins after that.

Sandra pondered what Jesus might have waiting for her in Heaven. It might be something special that He will want to share with her first and then allow her to share it with others. It may be something to eat or it could be a beautiful part of His creation in space. It doesn't matter. She received God's promise and she knows He keeps His promises.

Hope For Healing

During her time of extreme sorrow, Sandra could not find comfort for the guilt she felt from not fulfilling the role she was meant to play in Elvis's life. Though God spoke to her through scripture, sermons, and tapes, she could not forgive herself for having been so unaware of what she should have known, especially since she had prayed to meet Elvis.

Now her thoughts turned to Elvis' role in all this. Sandra wondered what it was about her letters that had intrigued him enough to go through all the effort to arrange a trip to Glens Falls, arrange a concert to conceal his presence, and then return empty handed without seeing her.

She visualized him receiving the first letter without a return address or complete name. How did he respond to it? What did his friends say about it? They probably had some funny remarks to make. But somewhere along the line, the letters meant something to him. Enough to compel him to go out of his way to meet her. For the next three and a half years following his appearance in Glens Falls, she had been impressed to write to Elvis again. She had squelched the thought almost every day, believing he had not responded to her letters in any way. The 20/20 hindsight didn't help any, either. It only intensified her suffering.

During prayer one morning, Sandra was agonizing over the thought of Elvis not being in Heaven because of her disobedience. "He had tried to reach me. It wasn't his fault," she prayed "Isn't there some way for him to have another chance?" she cried. "O, God, there's got to be a way. Please let there be a way."

Suddenly, Sandra remembered that Jesus had resurrected people from the dead. Some of the prophets in the Old Testament had prayed and people were raised from the dead. Some of the disciples had recorded that they had prayed and God had raised the dead for them. Eventually, Elvis would be raised from the dead too. For the Bible states, "that there shall be a resurrection of the dead, both of the just and unjust" (Acts 24:15). And "Marvel not at this: for the hour is coming, in the which all that are in the graves shall hear his voice, and shall come forth; they that have done good, unto the resurrection of life; and they that have done evil, unto the resurrection of damnation" (John 5:28,29).

Everyone will be resurrected at some time in the future. The Bible is very clear about it. But there will be two resurrections--one for the righteous and one for the wicked. Revelation 20:1-6 describes a scene in which the righteous are raised from the dead and are placed on thrones to judge for a thousand years. In verses five and six it states, "But the rest of the dead lived not again until the thousand years were finished. This is the first resurrection. Blessed and holy is he that hath part in the first resurrection: on such the second death hath no power; but they shall be priests of God and of Christ, and shall reign with him a thousand years."

The rest of Revelation 20 describes the scene of Hell when Satan, the evil angels, and all the wicked are destroyed in the Lake of Fire after being resurrected to face their judgment. This is the second resurrection.

In great agony, Sandra realized that Elvis' life had not been in harmony with the teachings of the Bible. He had destroyed his body, the temple of God, with drugs. He had lived a very promiscuous lifestyle with many different women. His life had not reflected the power of God to overcome the sin in his life and become "a new creature" patterned after Jesus.

Sandra realized that God had been willing to trust her with Elvis to teach him the truth that is in the Bible. With his probable conversion, millions would have been affected by his decision, the Bible would have been studied by people to see why he had made changes in his life, and everyone would probably all be in Heaven by now.

Uncontrollable anguish and feelings of helplessness had been her plight, but now, Sandra hoped that God would answer her prayers and raise Elvis from the dead. He had the power. He would raise him from the dead anyway at some point and time. All she wanted was for Elvis to be resurrected before time ran out to give him the opportunity that she had not given him through her ignorance and lack of faith.

Sandra knew God had forgiven her. She had no doubt about that. She had lots of evidence from the things that were happening in her life. When reading the Bible, new insights were given to her by the Holy Spirit. She thrived on the spiritual teachings that were shown to her. The deep, hidden treasures of the beauty of God came out and she learned the lesson that Jesus taught to Simon, the priest, when Jesus told him the parable of the two debtors. He said, "There was a certain creditor which had two debtors; the one owed five hundred pence, and the other fifty. And when they had nothing to pay he frankly forgave them both. Tell me therefore, which of them will love him most? Simon answered and said, I suppose that he, to whom he forgave most. And he said unto him, Thou hast rightly judged" (Luke 7:41-43). Sandra had been forgiven so much. It was even beyond her imagination what she had been forgiven for.

Jesus had forgiven the unforgivable. Another soul had been searching for His truth, which had been imparted to her since childhood, and she had failed to follow the lead of the Holy Spirit to share what she knew. Not only Elvis, but all the others she had had an opportunity to present the truth to as well.

Passionately Sandra prayed for this resurrection to happen. She did not know how or when, but believed it to be possible. She prayed that Satan and the evil angels would be cast away from the earth so the Holy Spirit could work on the hearts of people more easily. Daily she prayed for these things. A couple of weeks later, an unexplained event caused a communications satellite to be moved off course. Sandra believed that one of the wicked angels accidentally hit it when tossed away from the earth in response to her prayers.

Sandra became dissatisfied with just working a "normal" job. She wanted to find a way to work for God. So she questioned, *"What can I do for You, Father? I missed the opportunity You provided so many years ago."* Then she was reminded of the story of Moses. He had killed a man then became a shepherd for forty years before God finally gave him a second chance to free the Israelites from Egypt. So Sandra believed that God still had a work for her to do too. She just needed to find out what it was.

Part III

Every Heart Has a Dream

Empowerment

After a month off, Sandra returned to work. But during her absence, she decided to leave Hudson Falls that year. Her effectiveness at church had been marred by the stories Frank had told to the members. She was unable to tolerate the extreme cold weather anymore. Scraping off quarter-inch thick ice from the windshield one morning Sandra muttered, "I'm not going through this again." And she had become passionate about making up lost time to God.

Sandra didn't know for sure what it was that she wanted to do or what God had in mind for her, but she was determined to find out. She realized that she had to go to Las Vegas and complete the trip that had been started over twenty years before. God had wanted her there then, so that was her destination. She told only a few people where she was going.

That summer Sandra attended Campmeeting for the whole week. She knew it would probably be her last one at Union Springs Academy. An anointing was announced for anyone who felt the need for it. Sandra had never been anointed before, but received one this time because she wanted all the help she could get for the future.

Lying on her bed that afternoon, before the anointing, Sandra knew she would need prayer for several things. She made a spur-of-the-moment decision to write a list of things for which she needed prayer and anointing. Sandra put the paper inside her Bible and took it to the anointing service, but did not tell the pastors about the list.

When the pastor praying for Sandra placed the oil on her forehead and started praying, she listened intently. As he prayed, goosebumps ran all over her. He mentioned every one of the things she had listed. There could not have been better confirmation that the anointing was approved of God. After the prayer was over, Sandra showed the list to the pastors and explained what had happened. She asked each one of them to sign the list and she kept it as a memento.

Campmeeting ended all too soon for Sandra. The day after going back to Hudson Falls, Frank said he wanted to talk with her about their situation. Sandra knew he wouldn't leave her alone until he rehashed his point of view again, so she resigned herself to let him vent and get it over with.

Frank and Sandra sat at opposite ends of the living room. Frank started by addressing the problem he had with sex and his approach to her when he wanted sex.

"My experience with women was at a cathouse in Germany. I don't know any other way of making love," Frank said.

Sandra looked him in the eye and said, "You mean to tell me that after thirty years of marriage, you can't learn another way of approaching me?" Sandra felt empowered to face and deal with anything he had to throw at her.

Frank had no answer for her. Sandra realized that his ability to manipulate her was a thing of past. No more would she fall for his pity act or need for sympathy.

"I am a child of God, and as such, deserve to be treated as a child of God. He had no right to treat me in the manner in which he had before," Sandra thought to herself. *"I recognize that now."*

Sandra didn't back down. Frank had nothing more to say and Sandra told him, "I refuse to be a prostitute for you anymore."

Preparations, Planning & Parting

The summer months were slow at work. School was out and Sandra had been transferred to another office. Around that time, Sandra became aware of her goal to start a non-profit organization, *Every Heart Has a Dream*, a name she chose while at Campmeeting.

Sandra sent away to the Nolo Corporation to get a book on how to organize a non-profit corporation. She spent the summer reading the book and getting library books to learn about non-profits and obtained the free 501(c)(3) application for tax-exempt status. Most of her time at work was spent planning and preparing for her future. Since she had already given her notice of resignation and there wasn't much of anything else to do while there, she felt justified in using the time productively.

In the meantime, Sandra held a yard sale to raise money for her trip. She stopped paying the house payment and the bills. If Frank wanted to keep the house, then he needed to get a job to make the payments.

Out of generosity Sandra had foolishly charged $1,000 on her credit card for tractor-trailer training school for Frank. She told him he was to pay her back when he could. He said he would. However, one day, when he expected to get some

money, he sat back in his chair, folded his arms, and said
haughtily, "I'll decide what to do with the money when I get
it."

At that Sandra leaned forward and answered stiffly, "I will
never do anything for you ever again Frank." He unfolded
his arms and looked at her like she was from Mars. When
he received the lump sum he was expecting, he did not pay
her the money. Sandra decided to take matters into her own
hands. Before leaving, she sold the bedroom set for $1,000 to
her sister Sharon. A few days later, Frank told Sandra she had
stolen the money from the bedroom set. Sandra refused to
answer him and walked away.

The day before Sandra was set to leave for Vegas arrived.
Shannon, her six-year-old grandson, sat on the stairs
watching her go back and forth with boxes, packing the van.
On one trip back into the house he said, "Why do you have to
leave, Gurney?" (Gurney is the name Sandra's grandchildren
use for Grandma.) Sandra stopped and looked at his sad
little face and said sorrowfully, "Because Grampy and I keep
fighting and I don't want to any more." She knew he wouldn't
understand all the implications of her trip, so she broke it
down into something he could understand.

With the wisdom and tact of a six-year-old he said, "Why
don't you just tell him to shut up?" Sandra sat down beside
him with her heart breaking. She put her arms around him
and held him. Sandra prayed silently, *What will happen to him
and his sister Amber? No one will take them to church. How will
they keep on learning about You, Lord? How can I leave them here,
knowing they won't have me to teach them about You?* In spite of
all her concerns, she knew she had to let them go into the
hands of Jesus. There was work for her to do and she couldn't
do it there.

Sandra and Shannon had always had a special relationship
with each other. She could tell he wanted to cry. Sandra said
to him, "It's okay to cry if you want." He sat on her lap and
hid his face on her shoulder. His curly blonde hair brushed

against her cheek. Then he sat up and handed her a little green plastic soldier.

"I want you to keep this so you won't forget me," he said.

Sandra hugged him and said, "Thank you, Shannon. I won't forget you and I'll keep this forever." They sat for a couple of minutes more then Sandra continued packing the van. Shannon stayed on the steps and watched until she was done.

Sandra's heart ached as she finished packing. If she had only completed that trip to Las Vegas so many years ago, none of this would be happening now. In her mind the *words "All things work together for good to them that love God and are the called according to his purpose"* kept repeating over and over.

That night Sandra said goodbye to Shannon and Amber before going to bed. They would be in day care when she started her trip immediately after work the next day. Sandra would not be coming back to the house she had built with Frank.

The next day was Friday, August 13, 1999, Sandra's last day of work and the first day of her new life. Her co-workers held a party and gave her some mementos. Coming out of the building for the last time, she went to her van. When she opened the door on the driver's side, a note and a piece of slate chiseled into the shape of a heart sat on the driver's seat. Sandra's heart leapt into her throat as she recognized the handwriting.

The note was written in blood and her stomach churned as she read it.

***

"My love, I will eternally love you and really honestly am sorry for doing and saying the things that hurt you.

Signed this day in blood to verify the truth,

Frank M. Bailey, Jr.

August 12, 1999

***

Frank was trying one last desperate attempt to manipulate Sandra into staying. The feelings she had were indescribable. They were beyond anger, frustration, and hopelessness. Feeling distracted, but more determined than ever, Sandra went to a friend's house and showed her the note and heart.

"You are doing the right thing by leaving," she said.

Sandra called a church member who was also a New York State Trooper and told him what Frank had done. He was only concerned that Frank might hurt himself. Sandra told him that would not happen. He didn't care that she was upset.

Sandra finally calmed down enough to drive and then left. Since she didn't know when she would see her family again, Sandra had decided to stop at their homes on her way to Las Vegas. Her mother lived in Schuylerville and was the closest one. Then she stopped to see her brother, Mike, just outside Troy. As she was leaving he asked her where she was going. Sandra told him Las Vegas.

He said, "Does this have anything to do with Elvis Presley?"

Sandra was surprised he knew anything about that at all, since the only person other than Frank and Priscilla she had ever told was her sister, Brenda, many years before. They had been sitting at the table in Brenda's home when Sandra described the night at the Paramount Theatre to her. Brenda hadn't said anything, but had a look of disconcerted surprise on her face as Sandra related the story.

Sandra said, "Yes." Mike didn't ask any more questions. From there she drove to her brother, Dennis's home in Connecticut for the weekend. While there they went boating, had a cookout, and just spent some time together. Dennis talked her into leaving some of her stuff with him as he said the van was loaded down too heavy to be safe. He would send it out to her later on after she had a place to keep it.

Sandra left his home on Monday morning, bright and early. He and his wife Sheila gave her some money and told her to be careful. They also told her if she needed anything to let them know. They would help her with whatever they could.

Sandra traveled through Pennsylvania and West Virginia, practically without stopping. The scenery going through the Appalachian Mountains was breathtaking and made the traveling pleasant. She stopped only to take bathroom breaks with Haska, Priscilla's dog, which she had brought along. She ate by snacking on crackers and nuts and made it to her first destination, a hostel, late that evening.

(A hostel is a house or building that has been renovated and filled with beds. The beds are in dormitory-style rooms. Men and women have separate rooms, but sometimes they are placed together if needed. It is less expensive to stay at a hostel for $12-$15 per night than in a motel which usually costs significantly more. Hostels have a kitchen, several bathrooms, community TV room, and provide bedding.)

Sandra had called the hostel to get directions earlier that afternoon. The hostel was located off the parkway just before the Georgia border. Sandra turned off on the dirt road and went into a great forest of pine trees. The deeper she went into the woods, the greater became her apprehension. After about five minutes, she saw the car of the owner. He drove ahead of her to show her the rest of the way. Sandra kept thinking about horror movies and how unsuspecting people were lured into seemingly safe places just to be killed—or worse. She hoped other people were staying at the hostel.

The road finally came to a clearing with a large farmhouse-like dwelling. Some dogs started barking. Sandra was afraid to let Haska out, but the man said it would be okay. Sandra took Haska off her leash and she introduced herself to the other dogs. Then they ran off into the woods.

To Sandra's relief, a family was staying overnight. She paid for the night then carried the things she would need into the house. The hostel part of the house was located upstairs and a set of steps had been built outside to provide access to the rooms. That way guests wouldn't have to go through the main house to get upstairs. Haska came back later and slept in front of the door all night.

Early the next morning Sandra asked the owner to take her picture in front of the house. Then she packed up her stuff, loaded Haska back into the van, and continued on her trip. Sandra made it to her sister Gloria's house by late that evening. She and her husband live high in the Georgia mountains. The view was breathtaking from the upstairs loft of their home.

They talked a little while and made plans to get together with Janet on the next day. Gloria, Janet, and she would go to lunch with Janet's boys, Stephen and Jeffrey. Then Sandra would go with Janet to her home for a little while. Janet would then drive her back to Gloria's where she would stay the night again, leaving the next morning. Everything worked out as planned and Janet and Gloria very generously gave Sandra some money to help her with expenses.

This concern and help was unexpected, but so welcome. Sandra wasn't used to the support she was getting from her brothers and sisters. She had been pretty much separated from her family since marrying at sixteen. Sandra had felt that there had been so much missing from her relationship with them that they were siblings in name only. When they took her in and cared for her so lovingly, she came away with a greater appreciation for them.

Graceland

Thursday morning, Gloria and Sandra had breakfast together. Then Sandra continued on her trip heading west on Route 40. This would be the road she'd stay on all the way until Kingman, Arizona. Late that afternoon, Sandra arrived in Memphis, Tennessee.

Memphis—the place she had wanted to go so many years before. The place she had felt so much urgency to go to and had not gone out of fear. She found her way to Elvis Presley Boulevard and drove to Graceland ... twenty-two years too late.

Sandra parked near Graceland and walked over to the building where tickets were sold and purchased one to go on the tour. Emotions filled her with remorse and regret. She struggled to keep from crying. Upon seeing the gate, she was surprised to see how small it was. She had imagined it would be much bigger and more formidable than it really was.

Sandra got on the tour bus with a group to go across the street to the mansion. *"If only, if only, if only ..."* kept going through her mind. She silently got off the bus and followed everyone to the front door. The visitors were instructed on how to use the headphones for the self-guided tour and then went inside. Priscilla Presley's voice on the pre-recorded tour told some things about Elvis. Sandra blinked back tears and forced herself to just keep on going through. She followed the crowd in silence. Distracted by guilt and remorse and half-blinded by partially repressed tears, Sandra didn't hear half of what was being said or see what was being shown.

Numbly, Sandra kept going, knowing if she had ever come to the gate when Elvis was alive and introduced herself, she would have been allowed to come in and meet him. He would have been happy to receive her. With his search for God and her impressions from God to meet him, his life would have been changed and he would still be alive.

The tour ended by Elvis's Meditation Garden. Sandra, afraid to let her sorrow and remorse be seen, walked up to his grave and agonized silently. No one would understand if she were to burst into tears and weep uncontrollably—twenty-two years after his death. Sandra was still concerned about what other people thought of her. *"Will I never get over that?"* She held the tears back until she was back in the van. Then sobbing broken-heartedly, she drove to the interstate and headed west on Route 40 again.

Sandra drove until almost dark and found a reasonably priced motel to stay the night. The next day she drove past Oklahoma City before stopping to spend the night.

That night, Sandra had a dream of a woman asking her about her story involving Elvis. Sandra struggled with what to do and prayed for guidance. Then she determined she needed to go back to Graceland and ask God to resurrect Elvis.

The following day she got back on Route 40 and headed east towards Memphis. She arrived late and rented a room at the Graceland Inn on Elvis Presley Boulevard.

Sandra prayed and then crawled into the bed. She had no strength and tried to sleep. The three days of driving had worn her out. Suddenly, an oppressive feeling came over her. She could feel an evil presence and knew Satan himself was in her room. She'd never felt such a feeling of oppressiveness.

Even when faced by the girl possessed in the church, this awful and intense atmosphere hadn't been present. With this overwhelming presence lurking nearby, Sandra clung to Jesus and prayed over and over, "Jesus, Jesus, Jesus." Then she knelt beside the bed and prayed some more. She wept and asked for protection. After a while the evil presence left and she managed to get some sleep. Sandra wondered why Satan had come into her room and why God had allowed him to be there. Oh, how she wished she had someone to talk to and help her!

Early the next morning, Sandra walked up to Graceland. Some people were already in the Meditation Garden. She asked the guard at the gate why they were there. The guard explained that the Meditation Garden was open from 7 a.m. to 8 a.m. if anybody wanted to go there. Sandra walked up the driveway to the garden.

She knew what she wanted to do. She knew why she had turned around and driven back all that way. She approached the garden and moved away from the others wondering. *"What would these people think if I asked God to resurrect Elvis? Am I supposed to ask for his resurrection? And, if so, how should I ask for it?"*

Then suddenly the words came to her. *"Oh God,"* she prayed silently, *"Please resurrect Elvis. It wasn't his fault. It was my fault that we didn't meet. It was my ignorance and sin that kept Elvis from meeting me."*

Sandra didn't know what else to do. She stood there in utter confusion and grief and began to cry. Before long, the security guard came and told all the visitors that they had to leave. Reluctantly and slowly, Sandra moved away from the gravesite. She walked back to the motel room, collapsed on the bed, and wept some more.

Sandra realized she couldn't stay in Memphis. She turned in her room key and got back into her van. She had to go to Las Vegas. Maybe there everything could be sorted out. Once again on Route 40, she drove until early afternoon. By three o'clock in the afternoon it was too hot to continue without air conditioning, so she found a motel and stopped for the night.

The following afternoon she passed the point she had reached just 48 hours before. The van's motor started cutting out whenever she took her foot off the accelerator to slow down. She only stopped to get gas and let Haska drink and walk.

Sandra determined to get as far as she could with the van. She didn't know if the motor would die, leaving her stranded before arriving in Las Vegas. The next day she drove nonstop for eighteen hours, except for necessary breaks. That night, after passing Hoover Dam and its surrounding mountains, she witnessed the spectacle of a valley of glimmering shimmering lights below.

As she drove down toward the lights, she thought, *"What will I do and where will I go? There's no one to meet me here. I don't know anyone. I've never been here before. God help me."* Yet, in her heart, she knew this is where she had to be. God had something for her to do and it had to be there.

Struggling to keep the van going, which had been stalling on the highway, she finally chose an exit. She let Haska out and took her for a walk while she gathered her thoughts together. Then she got back on the freeway and felt impressed to exit at "Las Vegas Boulevard." Shortly thereafter, she stumbled upon a hostel sign. Because it had already closed for the night, she stayed in a nearby hotel that evening.

Graceland Again

Monday morning, August 23, 1999, Sandra was officially in Las Vegas. After all those years of wanting to get there and wondering what it was like, there she was. After leaving the Thunderbird Motel, Sandra moved into the hostel. There was no place for Haska to stay at the hostel, so Sandra put her in a dog kennel for two weeks.

The next morning Sandra went to the van to get some things. Across the street was a painting of Elvis on the wall of the Viva Las Vegas motel and wedding chapel. In the painting Elvis looked like he was officiating at the wedding. A pang cut through her heart. She thought, *"I guess that's why I am here. Las Vegas will either kill me or cure me."*

Almost two years had passed and she was still unable to forgive herself for failing God and Elvis. Every morning when Sandra left the hostel, she was confronted with Elvis's picture, forcing her to remember how he had trusted her and tried to reach her six weeks before his death. Sandra knew that she would have to face the past if she was ever going to overcome it. Yet, she still felt that she deserved the torment. After all, she had offered Elvis the hand of friendship then wasn't there when he needed someone. She had betrayed the one that had accepted and reached out to her.

Even with all the exciting changes in Sandra's life, there were still the gnawing pangs of remorse and regret. Contrary to popular belief, they didn't get any better with the passage of time. In fact, they got worse. By October, Sandra decided to take another trip to Memphis again. This would be a quick weekend trip; she would fly there and back. The week before she left, an earthquake shook Las Vegas and even reached Tennessee. Again, hope sprang up in Sandra's heart that Elvis would be resurrected.

Upon arriving in Memphis, Sandra took a cab to the Graceland Inn—the same hotel she had stayed at before. She visited a church on Sabbath morning and after lunch there, she got a ride back to her motel. She spent the afternoon resting, reading, and praying.

Just before waking up on Sunday morning, Sandra encountered the evil presence that had manifested itself the last time she was in Memphis. She again called on Jesus and soon the presence left her room. Sandra determined to ask God to resurrect Elvis this morning. She knew the gate would be open from 7 to 8 a.m. After her morning devotions, she dressed and walked over to Graceland and up to the Meditation Garden.

Only one other person was there. The water fountain splashed merrily. Flowers covered Elvis's grave. Pictures and letters from fans from all over the world brightened up his tomb. Sandra stood, unsure of what to say or how to say it. *"How does one ask for such a thing?"* she asked herself.

Time was running out. It had to be now or never. The guard would be coming over to send them away if she waited too long. Finally, Sandra spread out her arms with her hands face up by her side. Looking up into Heaven she requested the deepest desire of her heart.

Audibly she spoke saying, "Oh God, please resurrect Elvis." Sandra waited. Nothing happened. The fountain continued to splash merrily. There was no rending of the earth and upheaval of Elvis's tomb. No miraculous power attended her request for Elvis to be resurrected.

In abject hopelessness and helplessness, Sandra sat on a nearby bench and began to sob uncontrollably. It was a good thing she had brought plenty of tissues with her.

There was a man standing quietly nearby. He came over and said kindly, "You miss him, don't you?" Sandra nodded her head and managed to weakly say yes between sobs. After the two talked for a few minutes, the guard came and said it was time to leave. They walked out of Graceland and went their separate ways.

Sandra returned to her motel and spent the day in resting. Later she went for a long walk around the neighborhood. She wondered what it would have been like had she gone to Memphis when she should have. Again the Scripture "All things work together for good to them that love God and are the called according to his purpose" played in her mind as she walked on the quiet streets near Graceland.

"All I can do is trust that God is in control and He will take care of everything" she thought to herself. *"He can bring good out of bad things."* Even so, the knowledge that Elvis had trusted her and had humbled himself in front of his audience trying to contact her still tormented her.

Monday morning Sandra again visited the Memorial Garden. She sat quietly looking at Elvis's home. In her imagination she could see Elvis and his family and friends enjoying the swimming pool and cooking on a grill. They would have splashed and pushed each other, she thought, clowning around.

Helpless, Sandra prayed for strength to accept God's not resurrecting Elvis the day before. Resigned, she left Graceland when the time was up. She walked slowly back to the motel, packed her clothes, and called a cab to go back to the airport.

Living & Learning in Las Vegas

Back in Las Vegas Sandra returned to the hostel. Living there expanded Sandra's horizons by involving her in situations that she had never encountered before. Her sheltered and protected life had left her still quite naïve though she was forty-six years old.

Sandra had been working as a temporary data entry clerk at the Pony Express Company and babysat in the evenings. When the temp job ended, the babysitting jobs kept a roof over her head. There were weeks when she had just barely enough to pay for her bed and gas for the van, but there was always just enough.

While babysitting, Sandra watched television after the children went to bed. One evening a program came on about the last days of Elvis. A man being interviewed said that Elvis had played *Unchained Melody* and *Blue Eyes Crying in the Rain* before he died. As she watched, Sandra remembered something Rick Stanley had said on the "Unsolved Mysteries" program, "Priscilla wasn't the love of Elvis's life."

"If Priscilla wasn't", Sandra wondered, "Who was? As he had become the love of my life, had my letters evoked a similar response from him? I believe I was on his mind that morning. I believe he took the extra dosage to try, in his own way, to reach me. I believe

that because he urgently wanted to meet me, having stood before an audience, as an experienced performer, saying he was scared. There was only one person in the whole world that would have understood that cry for help and that was me. Unfortunately, I didn't hear it until five years after he died. Even if Elvis hadn't felt romantic feelings for me, he still tried to contact me. My letters made that much of an impression on him."

In different ways, more and more information about Elvis was slowly revealed to Sandra that kept her beliefs about Elvis not only supported but became clearer and stronger. Soon a man would come into her life that would provide the impetus that would force her to delve into Elvis's life to find out how he really lived and what he truly cared about the most.

Mark

Sandra met Mark at the hostel. He was a tall thin man and had a vision of becoming a professional gambler. Although she didn't gamble, they became friends.

One night the pressure of her beliefs about Elvis weighed heavily upon her. She desperately needed someone to talk to. Since Mark seemed to be the most intelligent person she knew, she hoped he would be able to comprehend her dilemma. Sandra asked Mark if she could talk with him. They went for a walk along Las Vegas Boulevard and Mark listened as she tried to coherently tell him about this part of her life.

When Sandra told him about Elvis saying he was scared on stage, Mark said, "That's what people liked about Elvis. He was not afraid to be vulnerable." When Mark asked Sandra if she had any proof that his statement was a call out for help, she had to admit that she didn't have any tangible, or empirical, evidence. Unfortunately, she found no responsiveness from Mark, only skepticism. She was still emotionally alone and anguishing over the past.

Mark tried to get Sandra to contemplate dating, but she kept refusing. One day, exasperated, when she asked him if he was happy with his life, he said he wasn't.

"Then leave me alone. At least I am happy the way I am," Sandra said. But Mark started nagging at her again, telling her that she was wasting herself by not having a relationship with someone. Sandra looked at Mark and solemnly said, "My heart is buried in a grave in Memphis," hoping he would get the message and leave her alone.

A couple of days after telling Mark how she felt, he said something derogatory about Elvis. Sandra said, "Why don't you just get a knife, stab me in the heart, and twist it?"

Mark suddenly had a strange look on his face. He left her alone for a while after that, but then started harping on the fact that she didn't have any empirical evidence again. To refute him, Sandra went to the library and checked out the book, *Elvis Day by Day*. In the month of April 1974, Elvis had enough time to execute a trip to Glens Falls. She showed it to Mark and he said, "I thought you were sure about that happening."

Sandra responded, "I am sure, but you kept telling me that I needed evidence. This proves that Elvis had the time to go there."

Actually, Sandra became very grateful to Mark. For he was the one who goaded her to start getting books and reading about Elvis. She never opened a book on Elvis until 2002. When she did, it was with mixed emotions. She had avoided reading about Elvis, listening to his music, and watching programs about him on television as much as possible.

The first book she read was *Careless Love* by Peter Guralnick. In it she found substantiation for her beliefs about Elvis. He had been searching for spiritual truth. Sandra's grief resurfaced. God really had wanted her to meet Elvis. Reading Guralnick's book only strengthened that belief. Every Elvis biography that she opened said the same thing: Elvis was searching for spiritual truth. It was an integral part of his nature. Elvis wanted to know more.

Conviction, Confirmation & Capitulation

As Sandra read, she understood what it was that she could have given Elvis in his spiritual quest. Since she had had to fight for her spiritual beliefs from a child, she would have told Elvis, "You have the right to worship God if you want to. Nobody has the right to interfere with your relationship with God. We have laws in this country that protect your right to believe and worship according to the dictates of your conscience. You do not owe your fans or anyone else your eternal salvation."

This would have encouraged him to pursue his spiritual longings. Sandra would have supported his decision to stop performing for his fans if he wanted to. She would have encouraged his desire to become a teacher for God as he told Lucy deBarbin in *Are You Lonesome Tonight?*

In Sandra's own life, she had married a man that didn't want to be spiritual. He went to church only to impress her. After they were married, he didn't want to go at all. Sandra wanted and needed a strong spiritual man in her life. She believed Elvis and she would have complemented each other spiritually. God knew that and tried to get them together.

Some would ask why God didn't overrule the situation so they would meet. We must remember that God uses faulty human beings to do His work. He knew Sandra would fail in this situation. He knew she was fearful of unknown things. Yet, He still impressed her to write to Elvis, which she did. He impressed Elvis to go to Glens Falls.

But there were other factors at work too. From reading the biographies, Sandra recognized that the men with Elvis would pick and choose the women that were allowed to get close to him. For whatever reason, those men outside Sandra's door talked among themselves and decided to tell Elvis something to keep them from meeting. They probably decided that Sandra was very young and might be trouble for him. She certainly didn't look like she was almost twenty-one at the time. If that were the case, then they were only trying to protect Elvis, which was their job. They were doing what they were supposed to do.

The sad part is, if Sandra had known that Elvis had responded to her letters, nothing would have kept her from going to Memphis to meet him. If she had the assurance that he wanted to meet her, which he did, she would have finished the trip she had started. Sandra was afraid, alone, and unaware of Elvis's spiritual quest, which she learned about after reading the biographies about him.

In *Elvis, You're Unforgettable*, Frances Keenan said, "All they (the fans) had to do was hang out in front of his residence long enough and they would eventually meet him and maybe, if they were lucky, they'd be invited in for a visit. Everybody knew this." No, not everybody knew that. Sandra didn't know that. Although she had been impressed to go to Memphis and introduce herself at the gate of Graceland, she had no way of knowing that Elvis would invite her in and would have been happy to see her.

Mark was more helpful to Sandra than he would ever know in her Elvis research. By reading the biographies, Sandra became even more convinced of Elvis's attempts to meet her because of his intense desire for spiritual enlightenment. Unfortunately, she also became more anguished over the past which she could do nothing about. She was caught between guilt and conviction.

Without any way to go back and change the past, Sandra pressed forward with determination to make *Every Heart Has A Dream* a reality. Though she had failed God and Elvis before, she was now determined to make her life useful to humanity. She could do this through her organization *Every Heart Has A Dream*.

Sandra understood what it was like to have low self-esteem. Her life had been lived in self-abnegation, always putting others first, leaving herself unfulfilled and empty. She could describe God's love and patience for people. She could tell them that God loved them so much that they were important to Him. Her own life would be a testimony to God's work through the miracles He had performed in her life.

Alex

As Sandra sat on the porch of the hostel reading her Bible, she was approached by a man who spoke with a European accent. She looked up to see a thin, handsome young man with thick, dark hair. He introduced himself as Alexandru and engaged Sandra in conversation. He told her he was from Romania. She had heard of Romania, but didn't have a clue where it was in relation to other European countries.

Being a "typical" citizen of the United States, Sandra was very ignorant of the European Community. That would change through her friendship with Alex. A lot of things would be opened to her mind during the next couple of years—things she never would have thought, experienced, or tried if she hadn't moved to Las Vegas.

As their friendship progressed, they spent more and more time together. Since they were both living on a tight budget, they had discovered the one-dollar breakfast served 24 hours a day at certain casinos. They looked for work together and located the Chamber of Commerce, where free local telephone calls were available.

Eventually, Alex ran out of money, so Sandra let him sleep in her van at night so he wouldn't have to be on the street.

After a couple of days doing that, he used the return part of his roundtrip bus ticket to go back to California.

A couple of months later, Alex returned to Las Vegas and stayed at the hostel again. Sandra was glad to see him. She wasn't used to people coming and going in and out of her life. They had formed a good friendship and enjoyed each other's company.

By December it was too cold in the hostel for Sandra to be comfortable. Alex suggested they get a room together somewhere else, but Sandra balked at that idea. The Bible states, "Abstain from all appearance of evil" (I Thessalonians 5:22). Sandra didn't want to give anyone the idea that she was engaging in sex with someone. By moving in together, that would be the first thing on everyone's mind.

However, the cold finally drove her to give in. She gave Alex some money to find a room they could share. Sandra was working as a babysitter in the evenings and Alex had started working at the Paris Hotel at night, so she knew he would be able to pay his share of the rent. That evening Alex escorted her to the Todd Motor Motel on Las Vegas Boulevard and showed her the room he had rented.

There was one king-size bed in the room. Since Alex still had one more night paid for at the hostel, Sandra was delighted to have the room to herself the first night. It was great! She had a shower in a warm bathroom and then watched a little television without having to ask anyone else if she could.

The next night, Alex moved in. He said he didn't mind sharing the bed with Sandra. However, she flatly stated that she would not sleep with him in the bed even if she had to sleep on the floor. Sandra had set up the twin-size bed frame she got out of her storage unit, but didn't have a box spring and mattress for it. Alex did the gentlemanly thing and slept on the floor in his sleeping bag. The next day, Sandra bought a box spring, a mattress set, and some sheets. That way they both had a bed to sleep in.

Sandra and Alex shared a motel room for about three months. Eventually, she became attracted to Alex for several reasons. Whenever they had a problem, he'd talk to her about it. Unlike Frank, he didn't get mad and put her down. He'd just say he wanted to talk to her. Sandra actually felt like a real person around him. He'd listen to her side as well as express his own feelings and he would admit it when something was his own misunderstanding.

Sandra felt sympathetic towards Alex because he wanted to become a citizen of the United States very badly. She had been thinking about them as a couple. Sandra's weight did not prevent Alex from being physically attracted to her. (Although Sandra had lost over ninety pounds over the last two years, she was still somewhat overweight.)

Alex and Sandra were talking one evening. He was lying on his bed and she was sitting on hers. The TV was on and Sandra decided to let Alex know how she felt about him.

"I love you, Alex." Sandra said. He looked up at her with his eyes wide and dark.

"How do you mean that?" Alex asked.

"I love you," Sandra replied. Alex didn't say anything more then, but his dark eyes intently studying her brought a flutter to her heart. She hoped he felt some kind of affection in return.

Soon after revealing her feelings, she slipped into bed, said good night, and asked Alex to turn up the heat. Instead of turning up the heat Alex said, "I'm coming over to your bed."

"Oh boy," Sandra thought, *"I've gotten into trouble this time."*

"No, Alex," she said.

Alex said coyly, "I am counting to thirty and then I am getting into bed with you."

Sandra repeated firmly, "No, Alex."

"This isn't what I had in mind," she thought, feverishly trying to find a way out of the predicament she had brought upon herself.

Alex counted to thirty. Sandra's back was turned to him, but she could hear him getting out of his bed. The next thing she knew, he was climbing in.

Sandra emphatically said again, "No, Alex."

Alex put his arms around her. Instinctively, her hands caught his and she held them so he couldn't touch her. Her heart was pounding like crazy in her chest. *"Oh, God,"* she prayed, *"What do I do now?"* This wasn't the outcome she had expected or wanted. In spite of the attraction she had for Alex, she wasn't prepared to have sex with him.

As soon as she prayed, God told her what to say. Very calmly Sandra said, "Alex." then paused.

"What?"

"This could be considered rape," she answered slowly and deliberately yet gently. After all, she had opened the door that led to this predicament.

Alex said, as if thinking out loud, "And then what?" He thought about it for a moment, got out of her bed, and then went back to his.

Every muscle in Sandra's body had been tense. When Alex left her bed, she was overcome with relief yet her heart still pounded as if she had run a marathon. After she finally calmed down, she realized she had become very warm. 'Thank you, Alex," she said.

"For what?" Alex mumbled

"Now I'm nice and warm," she replied.

"You're welcome," he mumbled.

Sandra was very careful about what she said to Alex after that. She had hoped that he felt the same way about her, but realized that he wasn't interested in her as anything except a friend, which ended up being for the best. A little while later, Alex met a woman from Florida and he moved there to be with her. He claimed he was very much in love with her. Sandra was so thankful and glad to be rescued by her loving Lord from her own folly and avoided having sex with Alex.

Priscilla

Christmas week Priscilla came to visit her mother in Las Vegas. She and Sandra shared the king-size bed while she was there visiting. Sandra had to work, so Alex and another friend, Peter, met Priscilla at the airport. They hit it off right away. That weekend, Priscilla, Alex, and Sandra drove her van to Los Angeles. Alex had lived there for a while and knew his way around. They spent the day going through Chinatown and seeing some of the local sights as well as the ocean and beach.

As Sandra walked on the beach, she couldn't help but wonder if she would have walked there with Elvis if she had completed her trip so many years before. In a bittersweet mood, she watched the waves on the beach as she looked upon the Pacific Ocean for the first time.

Priscilla stayed for a week. When Alex and Sandra weren't working, they were entertaining and showing her all around the casinos and the city. On Sabbath after church, they went to Red Rock Canyon and climbed around. Sandra introduced Priscilla to some of her other friends. Priscilla took lots of pictures and went back to New York all excited about her visit.

After Priscilla left, things went back to normal. Sandra was still doing odd babysitting jobs. The kids liked her because she would play games and do imaginative things with them. Dave, the owner of the agency Sandra worked through, kept getting requests for her from the parents for whom she babysat. She'd tell the kids, "If you'd like me to sit with you, tell your Mom and Dad to ask for me when they go out again." Then she'd give the parents a card with her name on it. She had quite a few repeat jobs and became Dave's most requested sitter.

Organizational Dreaming & Daring

In due time, Sandra incorporated *Every Heart Has A Dream* in the State of Nevada. She worked on the organizational paperwork and continued to learn about non-profits in her spare time. On her days off she looked for buildings that might be appropriate for the organization and found one that was perfect downtown. She called the realtor and requested a walk-through. Her friend Peter agreed to go with her to look at the building.

They arrived early and waited across the street for the realtor. Two men approached asking for fifty cents to get some food. As Sandra dug around in her purse, one of them said, "You have a glow around you." Sandra was surprised, but thanked him for the comment as she handed him the fifty cents. Again, God had spoken through a stranger to encourage her to keep forging ahead with her plans for *Every Heart Has A Dream*.

When the realtor led Sandra and Peter through the building, Sandra realized it would be the perfect place to work. On the outside a huge sign read, "Your future starts here." However, without money, it would have to wait. So she prayed that God would keep the building from selling until she could find a way to afford it.

There was another special person that encouraged Sandra, probably without his even knowing it. A homeless man, Ben, lived next to the hostel on Las Vegas Boulevard in an old, abandoned shed. Ben said he had permission from the owner to live there. He kept the chain link fence locked and he had a key to go in and out.

Ben would see Sandra coming and she'd stop to talk with him. He had a poem that used all the different colors and described the person who wore them with a characteristic or some quality they possessed. The final line to the poem went, "She who wears purple, gray, and brown will one day own Las Vegas town." Sandra found it quite amusing because she wore a soft gray jacket with a purple collar and carried a brown purse.

She said to Ben kiddingly, "What would I do if I owned Las Vegas? I don't smoke, gamble, or drink." He'd then go on to talk about what Las Vegas used to be like and how he missed the way it used to be. Sandra knew he was harmless and enjoyed talking with him. There were (and still are) a lot of homeless people in Las Vegas. She hoped to be able to work with some of them through *Every Heart Has A Dream,* helping them discover and pursue their lost dreams and aspirations.

Settling Down

Eventually, Sandra hired herself to a family as a nanny. Working as a nanny finally gave Sandra the financial freedom she needed to get her own motel room. She spoke with the manager who rented her a room when one became available.

In the spring Priscilla came to visit again. After this trip she decided to move to Las Vegas. Sandra was glad she wanted to be with her; however, it caused some concern as she was still living in the motel. They would need a real home if Priscilla was going to move in with her. In His providence, God had a plan all ready.

One day when Sandra parked her van during a trip to K-mart, a man approached and asked to wash the windows. Sandra agreed. When she came out of the store, she offered him a ride to his home, which was in a mobile home park. Several homes had for-sale signs on them. Sandra had never thought of buying a mobile home and probably wouldn't have if she hadn't given the man a ride home.

The day after signing the agreement to buy the mobile home, Sandra received an obscene phone call at the motel. It was definitely time to move on. God was orchestrating her life in His own inimitable way.

Priscilla arrived two months later in August, just one year

after Sandra had moved to Las Vegas. She obtained a job as a nanny within a couple of weeks.

Soon Sandra started working on the 501(c)(3) application in her spare time to get tax-exempt status for *Every Heart Has A Dream, Inc.* By the time she completed the paperwork, she had the $500 application fee to go with it. The day she received the non-profit acceptance letter, she danced around the living-room floor shouting, "Oh yeah, oh yeah, oh yeah."

Overcoming Fear

Meanwhile, back in New York, Cassandra had met another man and became pregnant with his child. Sandra asked for a month off from her nanny job to be with her daughter when she gave birth and was given a leave of absence without pay. She had been at the births of her other two grandchildren and felt it necessary to be there for this one too.

Shannon and Amber were thrilled to see their Gurney. She stayed in the upstairs bedroom that had once been Priscilla's in the house Frank and she had built. Cassandra still lived in the apartment added on to the house. Sandra was allowed in the delivery room and everything went well with the birth.

A few days after Cassandra came home, some friends visited with her and Bruce, her boyfriend. Sandra had agreed to watch Shannon and Amber. During the evening, after Shannon and Amber were in bed, Sandra heard some quarreling downstairs in Cassandra's apartment. Sandra knocked on the door and heard Bruce tell her to go away.

Sandra heard Cassandra crying and realizing Bruce was drunk, she went down into the apartment to see what was going on. Sandra managed to get between them by standing at the door of the bedroom. Cassandra was in the bedroom and Bruce was in the living room. Because Bruce was on probation, Sandra wasn't too worried about him becoming violent. He kept yelling and Cassandra kept crying. Eventually, Sandra found out what the problem was. Cassandra had asked Bruce to stop drinking, but he refused.

"And how did that make you feel?" Sandra asked Cassandra. Cassandra tried to explain. Sandra reworded her answer, "It made you feel like the beer was more important to Bruce than you were, didn't it?"

"Yes," she answered with her face reflecting surprise that her mother understood how she felt.

Suddenly Bruce was in Sandra's face, his nose touching hers, glaring at her eyeball to eyeball. He yelled some obscenities at her, but Sandra didn't flinch and stood there toe to toe with him.

"Go ahead, Bruce, hit me," she said calmly.

It was a calculated risk. She didn't believe he would.

"No, I'm not going to hit you," he said. He finally calmed down and actually apologized for his actions. Sandra accepted his apology and went back upstairs after Cassandra said she would be okay.

On the way up, she walked past Frank who had been standing nearby yet hadn't interfered in any way. Sandra knew that she had responded to the situation at hand instead of reacting to it. It was all part of the changes occurring within her. There had been absolutely no fear in her at all during the whole incident, which filled her with wonder. She had lived a fearful life for so long that standing up to this inebriated ex-con was nothing short of miraculous. When she said her prayers that night she thanked God for working in her life and making changes.

Miracles

In May Cassandra moved to Las Vegas with Bruce and the children. Sandra was glad they would be near her again and grateful to be given the opportunity to be a spiritual influence in their lives.

That August Sandra returned to Hudson Falls to help Frank clean out the house and have a yard sale. The mortgage was being foreclosed and he had to get out.

When she arrived, the weather forecast threatened rain. Sandra fasted for three days from Wednesday through Friday. She prayed that no rain would fall until after they closed up the yard sale on Friday for the Sabbath. Every day she'd look out the window and then tell Sharon, who had come to help out, "We can set up today."

Just after they closed up the yard sale late Friday afternoon, it started raining. It rained all night and most of the Sabbath. The sun came out again on Sunday, so they could sell some more stuff.

Just before leaving the following week, Sandra had a short talk with Frank. He was still hoping they could reconcile, even though she'd divorced him a year and a half before. She said to him, "Frank, I apologize for not being the wife I should have been. There's nothing I can do about it now.

We can't get back together. You see, I love Elvis Presley." That was the first time she had been able to actually verbalize her feelings about Elvis albeit her reason for expressing them at that time was so that Frank would give up on the idea of reconciliation.

Frank expostulated, "Elvis is dead!"

Sandra responded patiently, "Yes, Frank, I know that. I've prayed about it and prayed about it and tried to get over it. There's nothing I can do."

Frank looked at her and said nothing more. Sandra gave him a hug and said, "I'm sorry."

Although Sandra wanted to stay a couple more days to spend some time with her mother, she felt impressed to leave on her scheduled flight date. She flew back to Las Vegas on September 9, 2001. Two days later one of the most heinous acts of all time occurred on September 11, when terrorists flew into the World Trade Center. God had kept her safe from the terrorist attack by impressing her to leave New York when she did.

Sandra realized that she was listening to God much better than she had in the past. She recognized and followed the quiet impressions of the Holy Spirit more than she had before and it was becoming easier to recognize and respond to Him.

Reading about Elvis

After leaving her nanny position, Sandra was hired as a home health aide to care for an elderly man named George. The work was easy and the pay was good, but she felt as if she was wasting time. Working twelve hours a day, four days a week wasn't helping her get any closer to making *Every Heart Has A Dream* a reality.

While working in George's home, goaded by Mark to get proof of Elvis's intentions, she finally checked out some Elvis biographies from the library. She didn't know what she would learn, but knew it was time to find out if the things she believed could possibly be true. The more she read, the more she was convicted that Elvis would have welcomed her into his home and that her fears had been groundless. Sandra thought, *"He would not have allowed anyone to hurt me. He wasn't the sex-crazed person he was made out to be. He was looking for what others are looking for—a way to fill the void in our hearts."* Sandra became even more distressed over the shame of her past mistakes.

The A&E channel aired another documentary on the last days of Elvis. Sandra watched as the actor portrayed Elvis's eating habits during his last days. The program suggested he would eat fatty foods because he was reared on Southern comfort food as a child, but Sandra knew different. Elvis had been numbing his pain by using food as an analgesic.

Scientific studies have proven that when someone overeats, a large quantify of blood leaves the brain and goes to the stomach to help digest the food. When that happens, the brain becomes numb and thought processes become dazed. Elvis was eating himself into oblivion, just as a drunkard turns to alcohol, to forget his pain and misery.

In his book *Good Rockin' Tonight*, Elvis's road manager Joe Esposito stated that "his poor condition depressed him (Elvis) so much that he had to take more drugs and eat more junk to forget." As she thought about the suffering Elvis had gone through, Sandra's sorrow, remorse, and regret intensified.

Sandra could relate to overeating to escape emotional pain as she had done that herself for many years during her unhappy marriage. The food numbed her conscience when fantasizing about Elvis. It also gave her comfort when nobody else wanted to comfort or care for her. Likewise, there was no one in his life who could understand his pain, so he covered it up with food.

After reading some Elvis biographies that gave her proof of Elvis's search for spirituality, and knowing that God wanted her to meet him, Sandra became overwhelmed with grief. She had to go to Memphis to try to find a way to reconcile herself with Elvis's death, so she made another trip there in spring 2002. She fasted and prayed for two days before leaving.

Since Graceland Inn was close to Graceland, Sandra stayed there again. The next day at the Meditation Garden, Sandra started weeping. It was cool and she had on a hooded jacket. The hood was up and she stood near the wall so others could get by. As she wept, the people filed by silently--seemingly in respect for her grief.

After a few minutes, a gentle touch on her sleeve was followed by a young girl asking, "Are you all right?"

Sandra answered softly, staying hidden under her hood, "I will be, thank you."

"Did you know him?" asked the teenager.

"He responded to some letters I wrote him," Sandra said.

The girl was with two other young girls and they too were concerned about Sandra.

One asked, "Did you ever kiss him?"

Sandra's mouth curled downward sadly as she replied, "No."

The girls couldn't see her face. She kept it covered with the hood. As they were getting ready to leave one said, "I hope you will be all right."

Sandra responded softly, "Thank you, I will be."

How could she say to them that it was partially her fault that this man was dead? How could she tell them she didn't deserve their concern? How could she explain to them that her grief involved more than just the death of a man? He had accepted her offer of friendship and reached out to her, but she had been silent. Her grief became even more unbearable.

The books she read only deepened the guilt, remorse, and regret she felt. On top of that, she had no one to turn to--no one to talk with about why they had not met. No one to share her pain and bittersweet memory of a man who only wanted to make life a little nicer for everyone else. He believed his music did that. Sandra knew he would have changed his life if they had met. God knew it too. She would always be partially responsible for the unhappy ending of his life.

Sandra stood with bowed head and aching heart. She longed to change the past. The tears would not abate, but instead increased in intensity. As her sobbing increased, she realized that the others there were uncomfortable, so she left. She sobbed uncontrollably all the way back to the motel.

Sandra called Priscilla from the motel room and told her it was a mistake to have returned to Memphis.

Priscilla answered, "I knew that. What are you going to do now?"

"I can't do anything except stay here. I've looked up a

hostel and will be going there today. I'll let you know when I've moved," Sandra said.

God really did want Sandra to meet Elvis. If He hadn't, Elvis would never in a thousand years have gone to Glens Falls. The angel wouldn't have pushed down on her shoulder and head, urgently telling her to kneel, showing Elvis that she truly believed in God, *even though she did not know he was there.*

God had trusted her enough to have Elvis come to meet her, although because of ignorance, she didn't recognize what was happening at the time. Although she had prayed to meet him, she blew her chance when the opportunity to do so had presented itself.

Besides that, Elvis had trusted her too. At his last concert, he humbled himself, crying out to the one person in the world he thought could have helped him. And he was right. God knew Sandra could have helped Elvis or He wouldn't have allowed and orchestrated the many events that could have brought them together to take place.

Sandra saw Elvis's last film, in which he cried out that he was scared, too late. Elvis knew he had ruined his life. He was living in a nightmare and tried in the only way he knew how to respond to Sandra's asking if he ever got stage fright. Imagine the humiliation he must have felt working up the nerve to say he was scared; yet he humbled himself and did it, which was not easy for Elvis to do. In *Elvis and Me*, Priscilla Presley wrote, "He wasn't the kind of person who'd come out and say, 'I'm scared.' Instead I'd see it in his actions, his left leg shaking, and his foot tapping." Elvis must have been at the end of his emotional, mental and hopeful rope to publicly say he was scared.

After receiving Sandra's last letter telling him that she had reconciled with her husband and wouldn't bother him anymore, Elvis must have surmised that she hadn't realized that he had gone to Glens Falls to meet her. He didn't know what had gone wrong either. But he wanted to talk with her, if at all possible.

The next day during the Sabbath School lesson, a point was made that helped her release some of the responsibility for Elvis's death. Sandra knew and accepted that she wasn't at fault for the drugs Elvis took or the lifestyle he lived. She *was* responsible for not following God's command when he directed her to go to Las Vegas. She was also responsible for allowing herself to fantasize about Elvis instead of maintaining holy and pure thoughts. Had she not sinned, she would have been more susceptible to the Holy Spirit's influence and fulfilled God's purpose to meet and help Elvis to find the purpose in life that he so badly wanted.

Sandra realized during the service that she had believed that Elvis wouldn't be in Heaven because of his lifestyle. She had been judging Elvis all this time. Perhaps he had at the last moment of his life been forgiven before he died. Perhaps, like the thief on the cross, he had cried out, "Lord, save me." She didn't know and had no way of knowing. She did know that God would do EVERYTHING He could to save EVERYONE He could. And so the trip wasn't wasted after all. Sandra had to trust God that everything that had happened was for a purpose and that He was still in control of the world.

Walking through the streets of Memphis on Sunday, Sandra came upon a street vendor selling T-shirts. One that read, "God grant me the serenity to accept the things I cannot change, Courage to change the things I can and the Wisdom to know the difference" caught her eye, so she bought it. Although she knew the Serenity prayer, she needed something physical to hold on to. The shirt was four sizes too big, but Sandra didn't care. The prayer helped her put into perspective that she couldn't change the past, but that she had the opportunity, courage, and ability to change the future. Though she stayed in Memphis four more days waiting to take her flight back to Las Vegas, Sandra didn't go back to Graceland. There was nothing there for her to do.

God's Continued Leading

In Las Vegas again, Sandra became more determined to make *Every Heart Has A Dream* the viable organization she intended for it to be. She made arrangements to offer motivational seminars to the Clark County Detention Center inmates.

Realizing that she needed to be educated to carry out the objectives of *Every Heart Has A Dream,* Sandra started taking classes in social work at the University of Nevada at Las Vegas.

A week before classes started, she was impressed to resign from her job as a home health aide. The feeling that she had to resign came as a surprise to her because she had not long before made arrangements with the other aides to change her schedule so that she could keep her job while attending school. Sandra wasn't sure about the impression, so she asked God to give her clarification during the next Sabbath's church service. Three times during the sermon there were references made to employment and the need to resign from one's job when God calls one to do so. God gave her the affirmation she needed to let her know it was the right thing to do. That night she wrote a resignation letter, took it over to the house where she worked, and left it with the time cards which would be picked up on Sunday.

The following day, Sunday afternoon, the owner of the agency called to tell Sandra that she was happy to hear that Sandra was going back to school and following her dream. The owner also told her that George's (the elderly man Sandra took care of) guardian had requested that Sandra be discharged from the job. The guardian was miffed because Sandra had called George's son, who lived in California, to let him know that his father was slowing down and having more difficulty walking, as the son had asked her to do when he last visited his father.

Now Sandra understood why God wanted her to submit a resignation that weekend: so that she could resign before she was terminated. Leaving a job voluntarily is much better than a termination on a résumé. Oh, the wonder of God and His leading! Only He knew that Sandra was going to be terminated from the job that weekend. Even though she had failed Him in so many ways, He still was willing to work with her and lead her. Just as Moses failed after forty years as a shepherd, God gave him the opportunity to fulfill the plan He had for him from the beginning.

Sandra had learned that it is never too late to start over. For those who had a dream and lost it or those who are just realizing they have one, whatever is it, the dream can be obtained. With God beside her there was nothing stopping her from becoming what He wanted her to be.

God and Elvis had both trusted her. Sandra couldn't let them down again. She determined to make life better for others and be the person God would have her to be. She knew it would be difficult to go on at times, knowing that her mistakes and fears had kept her from accomplishing all she could have been up until that time.

She realized that she needed to encourage those who are living a double life to give it up and wake up to reality. For her life had become much richer, nobler, and more interesting since God had given her the victory over her sinful fantasies.

As Sandra read about Elvis, she understood why he had died. His death was purely accidental and unintentional. He never intended to end his life. Elvis died trying to contact her. His overdose was not an attempt to end his life, but instead an attempt to secure happiness and hope. Through his death Sandra found strength, courage, and an indomitable spirit. She found a man that wanted spiritual satisfaction so badly that he was willing to gamble with his life to obtain it. Knowing that, she promised to let others know about the ultimate sacrifice Elvis paid to obtain spiritual enlightenment.

Reality Check

Sandra believed in her heart that Elvis had formed some feelings for her. Just as she used her imagination about what it would be like to meet him and be with him, he may have been doing the same. In *The Truth About Elvis*, Larry Geller quoted Elvis saying, "It's my fault. I needed to love somebody so desperately that I read something into it that wasn't there." This statement was in reference to Ginger Alden, his last girlfriend.

Elvis wanted to be loved as much as anyone else did. However, his fame came between him and the love that could and should have been his. Most of his fans didn't seem to understand that he, and other celebrities, are only human. Yet, he was treated as if he were a deity, which is too much to expect of anyone. He, nor anyone else, should be held up to such expectations. Elvis was a man—nothing more, nothing less.

In spite of all the clamoring, clawing, and cleverness that his fans used to get to him, they dishonored, denied, and disregarded Elvis's true needs. Unfortunately, Elvis's needs continue to be dishonored even after his death, which has been hard for Sandra. For instance, one day when Priscilla and Sandra were sitting at a red light at Las Vegas Boulevard, a man dressed in a jumpsuit crossed the road in front of them. He crossed at the wrong time and someone blew a horn at him. After putting down the stuff he was carrying, he proceeded to imitate Elvis's movements in the middle of the street. As he did, Priscilla started laughing. Sandra was saddened by the mimicking of Elvis's persona in this manner. Priscilla laughed harder when she saw her mother's reaction.

Then Sandra said, "That is not funny."

Priscilla retorted, "Yes it is. What he did doesn't reflect on Elvis. It just proves that he is an imbecile."

Sandra sat quietly without answering. To herself she thought, *"Yes, it does reflect on Elvis. It is his image that this man is copying. How would Elvis have wanted to be remembered? As an imbecile in a jumpsuit making his stage motions in the middle of a road?"*

Elvis's life has also been used to give unabashed release to the inhibitions of other musicians. For example in the September 19, 2002, issue of *Las Vegas CityLife* magazine, Swedish rock group The Demons said, "We may be the originators (of rock 'n roll), but other countries have managed to expand upon a great idea in ways unimaginable staring out from the gates of Graceland."

In the first place, Elvis would not want to be associated with demonology. During his lifetime he avoided sects that did not follow the Bible or teach God as the source of spiritual enrichment. Secondly, the music talked about is not the same as that of Elvis Presley. Elvis never urinated on stage, destroyed his guitar, or used language in his songs that would be derogatory or degrading to anyone. Musicians like The Demons want to blame their excessive behaviors on someone else. Their reasoning is that if something is okay for Elvis, then it's okay for them too, which is not true. Even if Elvis had done degrading things, that doesn't mean others, who are responsible for their own actions, should. If the rock n' roll musicians of today want to demean, degrade, and debilitate themselves, that's not Elvis's responsibility. Today's rockers do what they do because they want to.

Sometimes ministers will mention Elvis's habit of having his bedroom windows covered to darken the room, suggesting that he was a sex fiend with nothing more on his mind than licentiousness. These ministers don't mention that Elvis slept during the day because he worked at night. Do these same ministers demean other workers that earn their living at night and sleep during the day? What if they, these other night workers, also darken their bedrooms so they can sleep? Does that mean they are only interested in having extreme privacy so they can be engaged in sexual acts?

When Elvis was alive, these preachers did not try to minister to him, yet they ridicule and scorne him without even knowing his whole story. Couldn't they see that the man needed and wanted help?

Did these ministers also believe Elvis deserved to be treated as a commodity? Would knowing that Elvis was denigrated and used as a means to an end give them satisfaction? Elvis was abused so others could benefit from his talents and popularity. In May 1977, when Elvis was on tour in Louisville, Kentucky, a doctor was "kneeling by his bed holding his body up and ducking his head into a bucket of ice water to revive him because Elvis was moaning and groaning.... The Colonel said, 'The only thing that's important is that that man is on the stage tonight'" (Geller). *No one deserves to be treated that way!*

The biographies are clear about people always wanting something from Elvis. When Elvis was home, he retreated to his room where he would not have to be barraged by people who wanted something. Like Ginger Alden's mother who hinted for him to give her material things and Elvis's aunt who flatly stated she didn't want to wait until he died to get money from him. Statements like these caused Elvis to withdraw from people, becoming brokenhearted and lonely. How would these ministers or anyone else like to live like that?

The rest of the people around Elvis pretty much had the

same thing on their minds: Get all you can while you can. The only interest they had in Elvis's spirituality was that because of it they'd receive more gifts from him. Elvis's guilt from bad behavior brought great rewards to those around him. Lamar Fike said to Larry Geller after Elvis gave everyone around a new expensive ring, "Well, Larry, I guess that spiritual stuff pays off after all. Just keep bringing those books around" (Stearn).

This way of thinking came across over and over again in the biographies Sandra read. Elvis must have become so discouraged by people taking from him until he had nothing left to give. It's no wonder why Elvis was willing to take a chance with his life to reach a person he believed could help him.

All these things weigh heavily on Sandra when she sees, hears, and reads about them. It is as if Elvis is no longer a human being, but only an example for ministers to use to further their own ends. It is true that Elvis's lifestyle was not consistent with the Bible's teachings. However, does that mean he must forever be used as an example of evil? What about his search and desire for spirituality?

"Sex and the acting profession have long been linked. This image of Hollywood, coupled with Elvis's constant need for female companionship, conflicted with his small-town-bred religious identity" (Whitmer). Elvis lived the life of a movie star. It was expected of him to be a sex symbol. We don't ever hear of anyone telling him it was wrong to live that way. His friends all encouraged him to party and carouse with women. It was accepted and expected.

Even Larry Geller, who was supposed to be his spiritual mentor, did not adhere to moral standards when touring. When engaging in extramarital affairs was he following the teachings of his perceived "masters"? Did these spiritual masters endorse and encourage infidelity? Their philosophy was intended to bring peace and enlightenment to others, not guilt and pain to oneself and hurt to those around them.

Was Geller living up to all he knew to be right? (Esposito, et al.)

In spite of all that, Elvis still attempted to reach out to someone who talked about God, quoted scripture, and offered friendship instead of immorality. Sandra will always remember him for that.

She will remember he planned a trip and a concert just for her benefit—a Christian music concert—when he came to Glens Falls to contact her. She will remember that Rick Stanley helped Bob when he had the seizure in the park and tried to stop her at the Paramount Theatre. She will remember the angel's touch and command to kneel at the conclusion of the concert and the angels that gave her money to encourage her on her unfinished trip to Las Vegas. She will remember that Elvis kept her in his thoughts for three and a half years and then tried to contact her in the only way he thought he could. Sandra will remember that God tried to get her to write Elvis again during that same three-and-a-half-year period following her initial letters. She will forever remember that she was on Elvis's mind the day he died and that he trusted her to respond to his plea for help from the stage.

Sandra learned much about Elvis's life in reading his biographies. In *Are You Lonesome Tonight?* Lucy de Barbin said that she and Elvis were lovers on and off for over twenty years. As Sandra read Lucy's story, her feelings for Elvis changed. In her heart she wished Elvis had been able to overcome his fears of what others thought of him, just as she was afraid of what others might think of her. He deserved to have true love in his life, just as everyone does.

Sandra will always love Elvis, but not in the same way as she did all those years while fantasizing about him. She gave him up to the woman he wanted to love. Yet Elvis still had a special interest in meeting her. After all, the letters she wrote were encouraging, although simple, and they spoke of spirituality. He probably also wanted to honor her marriage commitment by not contacting her after he knew she had returned to her husband.

The simplicity of her letters might have been some of the attraction he had to them. Elvis was drawn to young women whom he thought would be impressionable (Whitmer). What Elvis didn't know was the strength of Sandra's beliefs in God. That was why God wanted them to meet. God knew with Elvis's honest heart that he would have listened to the truths from the Bible and accepted them instead of using them inappropriately as he had been doing.

God knew that, much to Elvis's surprise, Sandra wouldn't have compromised the things she believed in like not eating pork and other foods forbidden by God in Deuteronomy 14, not wearing jewelry (Peter 3:3-4), and honoring the Sabbath and refusing to participate in secular activities during God's designated sacred hours (Nehemiah 12).

Elvis also thought of himself as a hero (Whitmer). He went to Glens Falls to "rescue" a maiden who had been beaten and abused by her husband, as his mother had been by his father (Simpson).

Most of the world knew nothing of his tremendous search for God until after his death. Elvis's dream for himself was thwarted through ignorance and unbelief. The Memphis Mafia didn't understand that God has only the good of His children at heart. Anything that He asks us to stop doing or start doing is for our own benefit. His entourage wasn't looking at the long-term picture. With God in his life, Elvis would have been healthy, happy, and hopeful. With only the material things of this world, Elvis lost his health, happiness, and his hope for understanding of eternal things.

Although he did his job by promoting Elvis, Colonel Parker also took away Elvis's hope of spiritual fulfillment. Parker didn't like the threat of losing money. However, the best albums Elvis produced were his gospel albums. These were the only ones to win Grammy's. Elvis would not have lost anything by adhering to spiritual matters and giving up the worldly. God will honor those who honor Him. "He honoureth them that fear the Lord," (Psalms 15:4). When Elvis recorded his gospel albums, the men who worked with him responded with overwhelming gratitude for his spiritual contribution when they were done. According to one biography, they had been affected so deeply by the songs, some of them were in tears.

His last morning, Elvis sat at the piano and sang "*Unchained Melody*" and "*Blue Eyes Crying in the Rain*". Who was he thinking of? Did he have any pictures of Sandra? Did he know she had blue eyes? He must have known. He was planning to take two doses of injections at the same time that day, six weeks after telling his audience he was scared while on stage. No letter had come then, so maybe if he were in the hospital, Sandie would write to him.

Larry Geller said to Elvis, "You are restless as well because you are searching for a mate, a soul mate at your spiritual level" (Stearn). Sandra didn't know that, but God did. God knew every attempt that Elvis made to reach out to Him. Unfortunately, Elvis was not being pointed in the right direction. He was filling his mind with "the masters" of philosophy. The books he was reading were telling him that there were many masters that he needed to study. Yet, Jesus said, "Why callest thou me good? There is none good but one, that is, God" (Matthew 19:17).

"Larry picked up a copy of *The Impersonal Life* and read aloud: For I am your real teacher, the only real one you will ever know, and the only Master; I am your divine self" (Stearn). Even Jesus didn't refer to Himself as divine, but instead pointed everyone to His heavenly Father, God.

Another time Elvis said, "Don't worry, I'm in control, I have *all the masters* (italics supplied) in my corner, counseling tranquility" (Ibid). His statement is actually contradictory to the teachings of the masters he studied because their philosophy stated that there is only one master—the divine self. So which is it: one divine self-master or many masters from many disciplines? Or is God the only good one that we are to worship? No wonder Elvis never arrived at any solid conclusions.

There is a statement in *The Desire of Ages* that reads, "The religion that comes from God is the religion that leads to God" (White). All these books on metaphysical and philosophical thoughts are not the religion that comes from God. Jesus said, "No man can serve two masters" (Matthew 6: 24), yet Elvis was trying to serve a multitude of masters all at the same time, which isn't possible.

It all boils down to fear. Elvis feared losing his fame and fortune. The entourage feared losing their livelihood and access to material goods. Colonel Parker feared losing his wealth. Larry Geller feared losing his position and facing scorn for encouraging Elvis to pursue his desire to change his life. Priscilla feared losing the man she loved to religion. The fans feared losing Elvis. Sandra feared what others thought of her and what her motives might be. And she feared the unknown. Perhaps the doctors, psychologists, ministers, and police feared censuring a famous public figure. Fear is paralyzing. No one should be that afraid of anything. For fear caused the world to lose a man we all cared about. And in Elvis's lonely decision to make himself sick enough to land in the hospital again was his last attempt to avoid death and find the life he really wanted.

Sandra had no way of knowing Elvis got stage fright before every performance. There was no reason for her to ask such a question. Forces of good and evil were at work. Good to have Sandra and Elvis meet and evil to keep it from happening.

Not only did Elvis say he was scared during his last concert, but at a previous concert during the same tour he said, "If you think I am nervous, you're right." And on June 19, 1977, in Omaha, Nebraska, Elvis said, "I'm going to do a song called 'Are You Lonesome Tonight?'" Then he added, "I am and I was" (de Barbin). It is of special note that he only made these comments during his last concert tour. He was sending out messages trying to get Sandra or anyone else who heard to respond. Unfortunately, they were messages that no one understood at the time because no one knew of his desperate plight.

All of Elvis's fans, friends, and family members would have found a way to help him if only they'd known how important his search for spirituality was. No one knew. Even the people closest to him didn't know. It took Elvis's death for others to realize the depth of his soul.

Doctors didn't know about Elvis's spiritual longings, but they knew he was taking drugs because he was in the hospital over and over again at death's door. His physical body was treated, but the spiritual part of his being was ignored. The police didn't know about Elvis's need for boundaries, which is why he taunted them by going into the jail while stoned (Esposito). Elvis wanted and needed someone to put a halt to his disillusioned lifestyle.

Sandra didn't know her letters had been received, accepted and believed. She didn't find out until years after Elvis's death. It wasn't until after she went to Las Vegas and started reading about Elvis and found that his spiritual quest had been documented in the biographies about him. Until that time, she had only the impressions that she had received from God about her part in Elvis's attempt to find spiritual help and hope.

"What did it all mean? Why had God given her these experiences? What were they for? How could she use them to bless others?" went through her mind, *"There must be a way to share what God has done for me."*

When she read in *Are You Lonesome Tonight?* Lucy de Barbin's question, "With such unequaled love and adoration, wasn't there anybody anywhere who could help him?" Sandra wept bitterly. *"Yes, there was someone who could have helped him, but she didn't know it then,"* Sandra thought. *If only I'd known of Elvis's desire for spiritual matters. If only I'd known of his response to my letters. If only I'd known…."*

And then she realized she wasn't the only one who hadn't known. If only we'd all known something could have been done. If only we'd known things would have been so different. The fans would rather have Elvis alive, happy, and with a woman he loved than dead. His former and current associates would have been relieved to have Elvis off the drugs and living his life with zest and interest. Everyone whose life Elvis touched would have wanted him to be happy and healthy.

Elvis wanted to have a life worth living. His last act was one of courage as he searched for the person whom he believed could help him attain that life. His legacy will live in Sandra's heart as she forges ahead with determination to use her life for others. Elvis did not die in vain. His spiritual quest will inspire and encourage others to seek spiritual truth. Elvis—if only we'd known!

Epilogue

Elvis's search for spirituality ended on August 16, 1977. He had fought against huge odds to maintain the beliefs that he had. Forced to keep on singing the songs he no longer wanted to sing, he quelled his heart's desire to keep peace among his family and friends. In the end, Elvis's deepest desire for spiritual fulfillment was denied.

Elvis truly embodied the spirit that God would have His followers possess. For they have through the ages been repressed, suppressed, persecuted, ignored, and forced to live the way others want them to. Elvis joins the ranks of those who were willing to "lose their lives in order to save them" for eternity. His life is a testimony to the truth that happiness only comes from being in conformity with God's ways and will.

Unfortunately, the world still thinks of Elvis as an entertainer and nothing else. An epitaph to him has been carved into the sidewalk, downtown in Las Vegas. It reads,

***

"Make no mistake
the city is aching for its King
his white jumpsuit spangled like a bullfighters.

In the city of thwarted loves
a million wedding chapels
would be dedicated to his name."
German Santanilla

***

If Elvis were to have a second chance, would the world still only acknowledge him as an entertainer? Would they give him the opportunity to live his life, unfettered to pursue his spiritual quest? We'll probably never know.

It is the hope of the author that wherever oppression of faith is found, Elvis's life will be held up as an example of what happens to people when they are repressed, suppressed, persecuted, ignored, and forced to live the way others want them to. Learning the truths about God would only have bettered Elvis's life--and the lives of his family and friends.

References

de Barbin, L. *Are You Lonesome Tonight* New York: Villard Books, 1987.

Esposito, Joe, et. al. *Good Rockin' Tonight: Twenty Years on the Road and on the Town with Elvis.* New York: Avon, 1996.

Geller, Larry, et. al. *If I Can Dream.* New York: Avon, 1990.

Guralnick, Peter. *Careless Love: The Unmaking of Elvis Presley.* New York: Little, Brown & Co., 1999.

Keenan, Frances, et. al. *Elvis, You're Unforgettable: Memoirs from a Fan.* Tampa Bay: Axelrod Publishing, 1997.

Nash, Alanna, Billy Smith, Marty Lacker, et. al. *Elvis Aaron Presley: Revelations from the Memphis Mafia.* New York: Harper, 1996.

Presley, Priscilla, et. al. *Elvis and Me.* New York: Berkley Publishing Group, 1991.

Simpson, P. *The Rough Guide to Elvis*. London: Rough Guides, 2002.

Stearn, Jess, et. al. *The Truth About Elvis.* New York: Berkley Pub Group, 1980.

White, Ellen G. *Desire of* Ages. Nampa: Pacific Press Publishing Association, 2002.

Whitmer, Peter D. *The Inner Elvis: A Psychological Biography of Elvis Aaron Presley.* New York: Hyperion, 1997.

Yogananda, Paramahansa. *An Autobiography of a Yogi.* Los Angeles: Self-Realization Fellowship, 1981.